Inspiring Peak Performance

Competence, Commitment, and Collaboration

Paula Jorde Bloom
Ann Hentschel
Jill Bella

NEW HORIZONS

EDUCATIONAL CONSULTANTS AND LEARNING RESOURCES

LAKE FOREST, ILLINOIS 60045

Design – Donna Jonas
Illustrations – Marc Bermann

Library of Congress Cataloging-in-Publication Data

Bloom, Paula Jorde
  Inspiring Peak Performance
  ISBN 978-0-9827082-2-4
  Bloom, Paula J. (Paula Jorde),
      Inspiring peak performance : competence, commitment,
    and collaboration / Paula Jorde Bloom,
Ann Hentschel, Jill Bella.
      pages cm. -- (The director's toolbox : management
    series for early childhood administrators ; 7)
    Includes bibliographical references.
    ISBN 978-0-9827082-2-4
    1. Early childhood education--United States--
Administration. 2. Early childhood educators--United
States. 3. School personnel management--United States.
I. Hentschel, Ann. II. Bella, Jill. III. Title. IV. Series:
Director's toolbox ; 7.

    LB2831.58.J673 2013   372.12'00973
                                 QBI13-600123

Printed in the United States of America

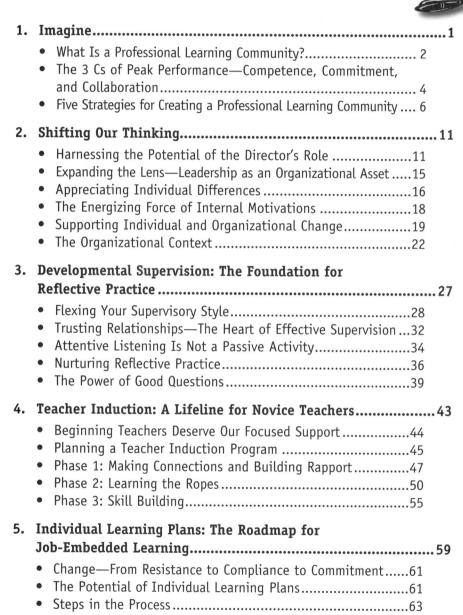

Chapter

About the Authors

Paula Jorde Bloom holds a joint appointment as Michael W. Louis Endowed Chair of the McCormick Center for Early Childhood Leadership and professor of early childhood education at National Louis University in Wheeling, Illinois. As one of the country's leading experts on early childhood leadership and program management issues, Paula is a frequent keynote speaker at state, national, and international conferences and a consultant to professional organizations and state agencies. Paula received her master's and doctoral degrees from Stanford University.

Ann Hentschel is director of quality assessment at the McCormick Center for Early Childhood Leadership, where she oversees the implementation of quality assessments and training of technical assistance specialists for the state's quality rating and improvement system. Prior to joining the McCormick Center, Ann worked for many years as a classroom teacher and as the director of an accredited early childhood program. She received her master's degree in early childhood administration from National Louis University.

Jill Bella is director of quality support for the McCormick Center, overseeing reliability training for the Program Administration Scale (PAS) and organizational climate assessments using the Early Childhood Work Environment Survey (ECWES). Jill works with state and local organizations providing technical assistance on how the PAS and ECWES can be incorporated into director credential and quality enhancement initiatives. Jill received her doctorate from National Louis University and both her master's and bachelor's degrees from the University of Illinois.

Acknowledgements

We begin this book by sharing a familiar scenario from our work as trainers at the McCormick Center for Early Childhood Leadership. While we do not currently direct centers, the training we do with early childhood administrators keeps us grounded. They are the ones who pilot the ideas we share from the literature on organizational development, change management, and motivation theory. For the last several years we've focused on helping directors create professional learning communities at their centers, integrating the strategies we lay out in this book. Their inspiring stories of individual and organizational change provide compelling evidence that the conceptual framework presented in this book is not an abstract theory, but rather a powerful template for encouraging individual and organization excellence. To these early childhood directors we are deeply indebted.

In writing this book we are grateful to our many colleagues at the McCormick Center who shared their ideas and provided feedback on earlier versions of the manuscript. A special shout-out of thanks to Safiyah Jackson, Donna Jonas, Robyn Kelton, Sue Offutt, Kathy Rousseau, and Teri Talan for the role each played in the process. As with the other volumes in the Director's Toolbox Management Series, Catherine Cauman has done a great job of editing the final manuscript. We are always grateful for her ability to fine-tune our work.

CHAPTER 1

Imagine

The scene is familiar, the discussion predictable. A roomful of early childhood directors has come together for the first day of a yearlong leadership training program. Full of anticipation, the participants are eager to talk about the challenges they face in managing their early childhood programs. Their centers represent the full diversity of the field—part-day and full-day, public and private, for-profit and nonprofit, Head Start, faith-based—yet the issues they raise are remarkably similar. "How do I motivate my staff?" "How can I encourage my teachers to be more committed to the field?" "How can I get my teachers to think beyond worksheets and cookie-cutter craft projects?" "How can I get buy-in to pursue center accreditation?" We've heard the same issues framed the same way for over 20 years at the training events we host at the McCormick Center for Early Childhood Leadership. No surprises.

In the leadership training we offer, we focus not only on the concrete strategies directors need for improving the quality of their programs, but also on helping them think deeply about their roles as leaders in creating the climate and conditions that inspire peak performance. You see, real transformative organizational change does not come about by checking off a series of tasks on a to-do list. It does not come about by reaching into a grab bag of motivational techniques to make teachers do more of this or less of that. True transformational change that inspires peak performance means thinking beyond employee-of-the-month motivational techniques. It means striving for something bigger.

In this book we hope to inspire you to think about what your program would look like if it were a true professional learning community—a place where teachers and support staff see each new day as an opportunity to expand their competence and confidence and support one another in moving toward a shared vision of program excellence. Before you can implement a program that inspires peak performance, though, you need to be able to imagine what that program might look like in action. What does effective teaching look like? What does a collaborative learning culture look like? What does supportive supervision and performance appraisal look like? If we can't imagine it, we can't achieve it.

Of course, our goal is not merely to inspire you to dream big. Creating vivid mental images of what you hope to accomplish is just the first step. You also need a few power tools in your director's toolbox to help make those mental images come alive. In the pages ahead you'll learn five strategies that together can help you and your teachers transform your program into a true learning organization. Most likely you're already implementing a few of these strategies but haven't thought deeply about how they build on one another. Before describing what those strategies are, let's first step back and define what we mean by the terms *professional learning community* and *peak performance*. We'll be using these terms a lot throughout this book and want to make sure that we've clearly communicated how central they are in the conceptual framework for guiding your work.

What Is a Professional Learning Community?

Educators are often the target of cynical swipes by the media and the general public for the jargon we use to describe the educational practices that make up our craft. *Developmentally appropriate practice, inclusion,* and *differentiated instruction* are just a few of the terms that sometimes elicit a puzzled expression on a parent's face when we describe our approach to teaching and learning. *Professional learning community* may well fit into that category; it's a term that is used extensively by administrators across the educational spectrum, but can still perplex those outside the field. In fact, the term has become so commonplace that it is now being used quite loosely to describe any gathering of individuals who share a common interest in education.

This casual usage of the term *professional learning community* troubles Rick DuFour, an educational leader known for his pioneering work in promoting professional learning communities in elementary and secondary schools. He fears that overuse dilutes the significance of the concept. The notion of a professional learning community is more than a catchy phrase, he stresses. It is a way of thinking that shapes people's expectations and behavior in an organization.

DuFour emphasizes that a professional learning community refers to the larger organization, not the individual teams that comprise it. While collaborative learning teams are an essential part of a professional learning community, the whole is greater than the sum of its parts.

So then, what exactly is a professional learning community in the context of an early childhood organization? Simply put, a professional learning community describes an ongoing process in which teachers and administrators work collaboratively in an intentional and systematic way to improve educational experiences for young children. A professional learning community is defined by the norms of continuous improvement, a culture of reflective practice, and a sense of shared responsibility for both individual and group learning. Professional learning communities operate under the assumption that programs are strengthened when teachers are involved in ongoing job-embedded reflection and learning. Continuous quality improvement is the mantra in such programs.

Take a moment to reflect on your own work history. Think of an experience with a group where everyone clicked; where work and learning came together with ease. What words come to mind when you focus on this memory? Why is this experience something you still recall to this day? See if any of the following elements of a professional learning community were in play with your experience:

- A sustained focus on learning, not just for children, but also for teachers
- An organizational culture that promotes collaborative inquiry
- Learning by doing
- Reflecting on action
- An unrelenting commitment to continuous improvement
- A focus on results
- Shared core beliefs and values

In examining the characteristics of exemplary high schools, Sara Lawrence-Lightfoot used the term *consciousness of imperfection* to describe teachers' willingness to look at their imperfections and create a climate of continuous improvement. That is the same mindset needed in our early childhood programs. At every level of the organization we need to ask, "How might we do it differently?" or "How can we do it better in the future?" You might want to begin to pose these questions to yourself at the end of each workday. Taking time to pause and reflect as you mentally close the door on a busy, demanding workday is the first step in cultivating the mindset for continuous quality improvement. "What could have been done differently today?" "What single small step can I take to improve things tomorrow?"

In her research, Judith Warren Little found that teachers in high-performing schools had strong norms of collegiality and their interactions were distinctively different from interactions in low-performing schools. Teachers engaged in frequent, continuous, and precise talk about teaching practices. They were observed regularly by their supervisors and received concrete and useful feedback. In these high-performing schools, there was time allocated for teachers to plan, design, and evaluate teaching materials together.

In the dizzy pace of daily routines in most early childhood programs, it is certainly not easy to carve out time for teachers to engage in deep, candid, and honest talk about the important work they do. The evidence is quite compelling,

3

though, that the frequency of collegial interactions is a strong indicator of a program's commitment to creating a professional learning community

The 3 Cs of Peak Performance—Competence, Commitment, and Collaboration

Woody Allen once quipped, "Showing up is 80% of life." If you've picked up this book, we're pretty certain the expectations you have for your teachers rest squarely in that remaining 20%. Our guess is you want an all-star team of peak performers—dedicated teachers who pour their hearts and souls into their work and take pride in a job well done.

Peak performance is another one of those management terms that organizational leaders toss around, sometimes lightly, sometimes seriously. In our case there is nothing casual about our use of the term. We are quite intentional in what we mean by peak performance. We're equally intentional about sharing the specific strategies we've seen that will help you achieve peak performance in your program. It all comes down to the 3 Cs—competence, commitment, and collaboration.

Competence is the "can-do" factor. When you review the résumés you receive for an open teaching position, your initial scan of qualifications probably focuses on each candidate's level of education, credentials, and classroom experience. These are good sources of evidence for narrowing the field of candidates, but they certainly don't tell the whole story about a person's competence. Competence is the unique blend of an individual's knowledge, skill, and dispositions.

Knowledge is what a person knows—the range of information a person possesses relating to child development, curriculum, teaching methodologies, inclusion, family relations, assessment, and so on. You get the idea. It's the content of what teachers learn in formal college coursework, informal in-service training, on-the-job experience, exploring the Internet, attending conferences, talking with colleagues, and even those pearls of wisdom tucked in fortune cookies.

Skill is the ability to put that knowledge into action through deliberate, systematic, and sustained practice. A teacher may read a dozen books and articles about different classroom management strategies, but not have a clue about how to translate that knowledge into practice when confronted with a dozen energetic three-year-olds all tussling for limited space in the block area. Skill also relates to a person's level of abstract thinking. This impacts his or her capacity to make informed decisions, solve problems, and fulfill the demands of a job.

Dispositions, while harder to observe and measure, are also essential in the competence equation. Dispositions are unique human qualities, a person's usual temperament. Lilian Katz, a revered leader in the field, says that dispositions are comprised of "habits of the mind"—the tendency to respond to experiences or situations in certain ways.

Some dispositions are absolutely essential for effective classroom teaching—empathy, positive regard for others, flexibility, a nurturing spirit. Other dispositions are essential for ethical professional practice—fairness, appreciation of differing points of view, respect for diversity, a sense of social justice. When we talk about creating a professional learning community and a culture of continuous improvement, dispositions for reflection, curiosity, lifelong learning, and openness to change are particularly critical.

It should be clear from this brief definition of competence that our knowledge, skills, and dispositions are under construction throughout our entire lives and have a significant impact on how we perceive and carry out our roles.

Commitment is the "wanna-do" factor relating to performance. It is the strength of a teacher's belief in and acceptance of a center's goals and values; in other words, a teacher's willingness to exert effort on behalf of the organization. In an early childhood context, level of organizational commitment has been found to be strongly related to overall job satisfaction, salary, turnover, and the degree to which teachers' perceptions of their current work environment resemble their ideal.

Every director occasionally deals with an employee with that intractable bad attitude; the one who never volunteers, who tries to get by putting in the least amount of effort possible. The experience dealing with such an employee underscores the point that competence isn't enough. Commitment, that wanna-do attitude, is essential for a high-functioning team.

While every director wants teachers to be fully engaged in their jobs and dedicated to the mission of their center, directors who inspire peak performance also want their teachers to be committed to something larger—the early childhood profession. They want their teachers to think of their work not as "just a job," but rather as a higher calling, a lifelong career in the field. Teachers who think of their work as a career are more future-oriented and therefore more likely to invest the time needed to expand their knowledge base and repertoire of skills.

Embracing this broader definition of commitment presents a challenge for directors who work in an organizational context of limited resources. Attracting teachers who have a career orientation is difficult when the salaries and benefits you offer are more in line with the fast-food industry, where a career orientation is certainly not the expectation. The good news is that directors who implement strategies to promote peak performance can often inspire teachers to begin to see themselves as professionals, thus fueling teachers' commitment to something larger than the next paycheck. More on that later.

Collaboration is the "we're-in-this-together" factor. Too often teachers work in their own little bubble. This can be true even within a teaching team, where there tends to be a spoken or unspoken hierarchy with designated duties. A true professional learning community is based on a core value that the whole is greater than the sum of its parts. That means creating the conditions in which teachers see one another as essential sources of information and learning. The collaboration factor is what distinguishes truly exemplary programs from good-enough programs.

The hallmark of a collaborative culture is a sense of community in which individuals are more than just friendly and congenial co-workers. Not only do they care about one another, they are interdependent and support each other's learning. True collaboration in learning is more than contrived congeniality—bringing in donuts on Friday or fun events that foster friendships and social connections. Donuts, fun events, friendships, and social connections are fine and dandy, but they won't move the needle in program quality. A true collaborative culture does more than promote friendships. It recognizes and rewards people's contributions to the *collective*—elevating the collective wisdom, expertise, and accountability of everyone. In the pages ahead you'll learn strategies to help make this happen in your program.

Five Strategies for Creating a Professional Learning Community

For most directors, the notion of a professional learning community is easy to embrace; it simply makes good sense. Making it a reality in an early childhood program, however, requires more than a superficial understanding of the concept and surface attempts at reorganizing. It requires a shift in thinking about your role as leader and a resolute effort to implement strategies that ensure that competence, commitment, and collaboration are woven into the fabric of your organizational values and practices.

We'll look at your leadership role in greater detail in Chapter 2. But here is a preview of what lays ahead in the chapters that follow: five strategies that together will help you transform your center into a professional learning community. These strategies should be thought of not as separate approaches for promoting peak performance, but as interconnected approaches that together reinforce the effectiveness of each other.

Developmental supervision—the foundation for reflective practice. In Chapter 3 we'll jump headfirst into a discussion of two of the core principles that serve as the foundation for a professional learning community—developmental supervision and reflective practice. We'll discuss how supervisory support can be tailored to the unique needs of each teacher on your team. You'll learn how attentive listening and good questions help nurture teachers' dispositions to be reflective and how the classroom can serve as a rich laboratory for learning and confidence building.

Teacher induction—a lifeline for novice teachers. Most beginning teachers speak of their first year on the job with a mix of colorful language straight from the reality show *Survivor*. As a profession we can do much better than the standard sink-or-swim approach that most new teachers experience. In Chapter 4 we'll look at how programs can expand their traditional one-day/one-week staff orientation to become a yearlong supportive experience for new teachers.

Individual learning plans—the roadmap for job-embedded learning. In Chapter 5 you'll find out why the one-size-fits-all in-service training that dominates most early childhood programs is doomed to disappoint. Instead, professional development needs to build on teachers' knowledge and the day-to-day challenges they experience in the classroom. In this chapter you'll learn how to individualize professional development experiences so they address teachers' strengths, interests, expressed needs, learning style, and career aspirations.

Peer learning teams—the platform for collegial support. When teachers are provided with dedicated time to meet with colleagues to reflect on their professional practice, they not only develop a deeper appreciation of the nuances of best practice, they learn how to facilitate and support the learning of others. In Chapter 6 you'll see how peer learning teams can be a powerful tool for building leadership capacity throughout your center.

360-degree feedback—a catalyst for growth and change. Traditional top-down models of performance appraisal not only create a climate of intimidation in many organizations, but stifle the potential for creative thinking and growth. In Chapter 7 you'll learn about the power of 360-degree feedback and how tapping into multiple perspectives in the performance appraisal process can strengthen performance and accountability.

The following diagram illustrates the power of these five strategies to transform your program into a vibrant learning community, one that consistently and thoughtfully focuses on continuous quality improvement.

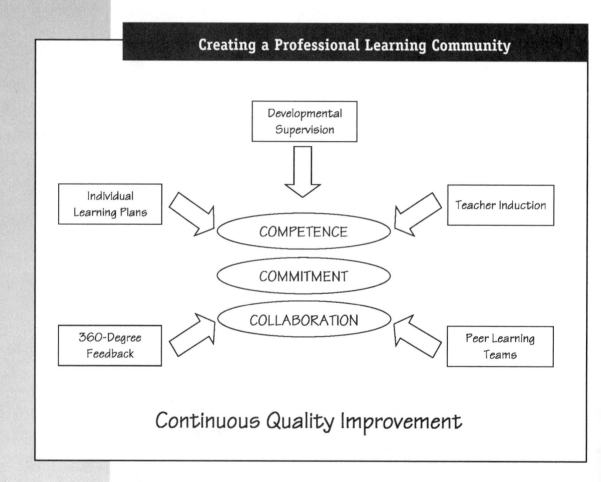

In this chapter we've asked you to dream big—to think about what your program might look like in terms of competence, commitment, and collaboration if you achieved your ideal. Now it's your turn to capture those mental images on paper by completing Exercise 1.

Try to be specific in capturing the elements of what teaching practices, collegial relations, professional development supports, and performance evaluation systems might look like if you achieved your ideal. Next, candidly assess where your program is now in terms of your staff's overall level of competence, commitment, and collaboration. By capturing the images of what you hope to achieve and realistically evaluating where you are now, you'll be able to see the gap between your current reality and your ideal. Jot down some notes about the areas that contribute most to the gap.

My ideal—what I want my program to be

_____

_____

_____

Whether you think that you can or you can't, you're usually right.

Henry Ford

The reality—where my program is now

_____

_____

_____

The gap—the difference between my ideal and where my program is now

_____

_____

_____

CHAPTER 2

Shifting Our Thinking

It may sound like a cliché, but it is true that change starts in the head. Whether you achieve the ideal you envision for your program depends in large part on how you perceive your leadership role. In this chapter we'll pose some tough questions to help bring to the surface the core assumptions that guide your thinking about how to best motivate people and inspire individual and collective change.

You see, a professional learning community isn't something that can be imposed or implemented by decree. To the contrary, it is a way of thinking and working together that emerges from a shared sense of passion and purpose. Its potential is powerful, but like any educational approach, it can be implemented superficially or with genuine depth that can transform those involved from the inside out.

This chapter lays out the foundational principles for transforming your program into a vibrant learning organization. We first look at the potential of the director's role as it relates to your goal of inspiring peak performance. This is important because how you perceive your role impacts every interaction you have with your staff. We then broaden the discussion, looking at leadership as an organizational asset. The next shift in thinking relates to motivating employees and tapping into each person's unique qualities to individualize supports. The discussion then turns to the nature of change in individuals and the importance of a strengths-based approach to supporting peak performance. Finally we address the issue of organizational context. Much of effective human resources management depends on the context in which you work. It is the variable that makes your approach different from every other director's approach.

Harnessing the Potential of the Director's Role

If you've been a director for even a short time, you are keenly aware of the pivotal role you play in your center's quality equation. Your teachers may impact children's experiences directly, but you impact children's developmental outcomes by structuring the conditions that support teacher effectiveness. The decisions you make related to hiring, supervision, professional development, and performance appraisal all influence the trajectory of your program in achieving excellence. Even routine decisions about teachers' work schedules affect whether teachers have time to work together to promote each other's learning. There is no getting around it. Virtually everything you do in your leadership role directly or indirectly influences the reputation and success of your program.

Let's look at your multifaceted role as the gatekeeper to quality to tease out the many ways your actions can inspire peak performance.

- As **pedagogical leader** you ask the deep philosophical questions that get to the heart of your center's mission. What is the purpose of education? What traits do you want children to have as a result of their experiences in your program? You are the one who helps teachers sort through the tough issues, like how to meet external mandates that often have a mind-numbing focus on children's future school achievement, while still providing a well-rounded approach to enriching early childhood experiences today.

- As **vision builder** you work with staff to translate your center's core values into a clear roadmap for reflective and ethical practice. Creating a vision is really about shaping expectations, both individual and collective. Directors communicate what they value and consider important through the things they pay attention to, comment on, ask about, and praise. Beginning teachers, in particular, take notice.

- As **talent developer** you make sure everyone has the time and resources for, and access to, professional development opportunities. With the general level of education and specialized training of the workforce still quite low, this aspect of your role is crucial. In providing meaningful professional development opportunities, directors cultivate talent and expertise from the ground up.

- As **data manager** you collect and organize information for accountability. More than ever before, programs need to document the outcomes of their work to funders, regulators, parents, and community partners. You recognize that collecting data is not the same as using data, so you help teachers use information about their classroom practices and children's progress to strengthen the loop of continuous quality improvement.

Before you are a leader, success is all about growing yourself. When you become a leader, success is all about growing others.

Jack Welch

12

- As **knowledge broker** you structure opportunities for people to share their experience and expertise with one another. This means being intentional about providing the time and the emotional climate that encourage teachers to become active partners in each other's learning. Creating the physical space for conversations to take place during the day is also essential if you want teachers to engage in ongoing exchanges that deepen their learning.

- As **systems engineer** you implement the policies and procedures needed for continuous quality improvement. Keeping track of scheduled meetings, assessment data, professional development opportunities, and resources to support learning requires big-picture thinking and well-thought-out systems to ensure smooth operations.

- As **idea igniter** you stimulate and encourage teachers to look at their classroom and organizational practices in new and creative ways. By regularly asking "What if ..." and creating the spaces and places for ideas to flourish, you can rev up your center's creativity quotient. Your words and your actions can turn the smoldering embers of complacency into sparks of creativity.

- As **cheerleader** you work to maintain a positive energy that encourages efforts and celebrates accomplishments. Validation and meaningful praise go a long way toward building enthusiasm and bolstering confidence.

- As **change agent** you monitor carefully how much "new stuff" people can absorb at any one time. This means being mindful of workload and the changes in relationships people experience as new ideas are implemented.

- As **CEO (Chief Example to Others)** you serve as an inspiring role model of lifelong learning and professional renewal. This means willingly acknowledging areas of your own practice that need to be strengthened, actively participating in your own professional development, and eagerly sharing what you have learned with others.

Take a moment to review the many hats you wear as you think about your own repertoire of leadership strengths. Which of these ten facets of the director's role needed to create a professional learning community do you consider as your strengths? Which facets do you think you may need to work on?

	Strength	Need to work on
Pedagogical leader	_____	_____
Vision builder	_____	_____
Talent developer	_____	_____
Data manager	_____	_____
Knowledge broker	_____	_____
Systems engineer	_____	_____
Idea igniter	_____	_____
Cheerleader	_____	_____
Change agent	_____	_____
Chief Example to Others	_____	_____

Similar to looking through the wide-angle lens of a camera, directors must be able to step back and see the big picture—the organization as a whole—to determine the impact of different actions. They must also zoom in on the needs of individuals and how they might react to any change. This means being able to shift from one perspective to another, viewing the same situation from different vantage points when making decisions, building systems, supervising staff, and evaluating actions.

Take a moment to think about your own tendency. Do you have a sense of where you spend more of your energy and focus? Is it on issues that relate to the organization as a whole or on the needs and concerns of individual people who work at your center? Do you find it easy or difficult to shift your focus when circumstances require? Recognizing and accepting this inherent tension in your leadership role will help you navigate some of the tricky situations that are bound to surface as you implement strategies to inspire peak performance.

Expanding the Lens—Leadership as an Organizational Asset

Thinking about your organization as a professional learning community requires a shift from thinking about leadership as solely the director's responsibility to thinking about it as a model of distributed responsibility in which many at your center share accountability. In this broader view, leadership is viewed as an organizational asset; an asset that is not fixed, but rather one that can be strengthened and expanded. It is a model where communication and development of new ideas flow from several directions, not just from the top down.

While many early childhood administrators readily embrace this broader concept of leadership, putting it into practice is another thing. Some directors simply have difficulty sharing their power, preferring instead to keep tight control over their influence and decision-making authority. Others are not confident that their staff can live up to their quality expectations. And still others are reluctant to share leadership authority because they worry about overloading their staff with administrative responsibilities when their primary focus should be on teaching.

The irony is that by strengthening a center's overall leadership capacity, directors are more likely to improve staff morale, build a collaborative spirit, and reduce disruptive turnover. Distributed leadership is essential for achieving the kind of organizational culture in which a professional learning community thrives. It begins with small steps—encouraging staff to take on small acts of leadership like mentoring others, facilitating team meetings, leading committees or projects, contributing to the center's newsletter, and analyzing assessment data.

Thinking about these ideas metaphorically means shifting from the typical hierarchical configuration (where leadership resides at the top), or even from a wheel configuration (where the center hub represents the leader), to a web configuration in which each touch point in the web is vital for maintaining the strength and viability of the entire web.

In this book we discuss several ways you can expand the leadership capacity in your center. You'll learn how collegial mentoring supports new teacher induction, how peer learning teams help hone teachers' small-group facilitation skills, and how co-worker feedback helps strengthen your center's performance appraisal process.

If you are interested in the idea of distributed leadership and wonder where your program stands in terms of its collective leadership capacity, take some time to complete Appendix A, "Leadership as an Organizational Asset." It'll provide you with a quick assessment of your center's leadership capacity as it relates to several essential skills and competencies.

Appreciating Individual Differences

In early childhood classrooms we readily embrace the importance of individualizing instruction, but when it comes to the supervision, professional development, and performance appraisal of teachers, many programs rely on a one-size-fits-all approach—that is, they use the same forms and protocols for individuals throughout the center, even if staff work in different age-group settings and have different levels of experience or career goals. This cookie-cutter approach misses the mark. Being serious about creating a professional learning community means seriously considering the unique interests, strengths, and needs of each person on your staff and individualizing your approach based on those differences.

Take a look at the list on the following page of the many ways that people differ. As you read through the items, think about the teachers in your center. How well do you *really* know them? How complete a profile could you develop for each person?

This list includes the competence and commitment factors we discussed in Chapter 1, along with a host of other personal traits and characteristics that help explain the enormous diversity we see every day in human behavior. These variations make a huge difference in the way people take in and process information, their inclination to modify their current practices, and their desire to pursue new goals.

In addition to the items in this list is another factor that has a bearing on people's preferences and worldview—generational differences. Differences in generation or age have implications for the way teachers approach their work, how they impact the culture of the center, and the kind of supports they need to be fully engaged. Think about your own center and how generational differences among teachers affect interpersonal relations.

Some of the Ways Individuals Differ

- Knowledge of child development, effective instructional practices, classroom management practices, and curriculum approaches

- Ability to put knowledge into action (for example, maintain classroom order, assess children's growth and development, lead a circle time, or console a child)

- Dispositions and temperament (for example, tendency to be nurturing, playful, curious, optimistic, flexible, resilient, risk taking, or self-starting)

- Teaching style—how knowledge, skills, and dispositions come together

- Work-style preferences (for example, likes to work alone or as part of a team)

- Physical abilities and energy level

- Adult development stage and career stage

- Cognitive capacity—ability to process abstract concepts

- Needs and expectations for autonomy, structure, variety, neatness, control, and intellectual challenge

- Interests and special talents in areas such as music, art, drama, literature, athletics

- Values and beliefs about education, such as appropriate goals for children, the role of the teacher, the importance of diversity, the role of parents, and the importance of inclusion

- Level of commitment to the center

- Learning style and sensory modality preference (visual, auditory, kinesthetic)

- Communication style (direct, spirited, considerate, systematic)

- Outside commitments and obligations

- Personal ethics and integrity

- Professional orientation—perceptions of work as a job or as a career—and degree of involvement in career advancement opportunities

Adapted from Bloom, P. J. (2005). *Blueprint for action: Achieving center-based change through staff development.* Lake Forest, IL: New Horizons. Reprinted with permission.

Many directors report tension between teachers from different generations, with older staff often dismissive of younger teachers. While young and energetic teachers have always been a threat to some older teachers whose enthusiasm and energy may be waning, today there seems to be an additional dynamic at play. Members of the youngest of the generational groups, the Millennial Generation, find security in fast-paced, high-connectivity environments and are often impatient with traditional communication modes or group meeting formats. It takes a savvy director—one who sees diversity as an organizational asset—to turn these generational differences into a positive force for change.

The Energizing Force of Internal Motivations

Working with teachers from different generations also provides a great example of how people are motivated by different incentives. Baby Boomers nearing retirement may be motivated by having greater flexibility in their work schedules or being offered opportunities to pass on their knowledge and experience through mentoring new teachers. Their younger colleagues, who are in the early stages of their careers, may be motivated more by special recognition, titles, and increasing levels of responsibility that acknowledge their budding expertise.

The point is that all teachers differ in their needs and expectations, and so do the motivators that serve as energizing forces to inspire them to strengthen their levels of competency and their commitment to the center. This means that directors should not ask, "How do I motivate my teachers?," but rather, "How can I tap into the unique motivational factors that make each person want to achieve his or her best?"

Drawing on four decades of research on human motivation, Daniel Pink, in his book *Drive: The Surprising Truth about What Motivates Us*, addresses the mismatch between scientific findings about the importance of intrinsic motivators and the way current work environments are structured. He argues that the emphasis on bonuses, merit pay, and other extrinsic rewards is misguided. Today's workplace structure needs to promote autonomy, mastery, and purpose if it is to fully engage workers and advance their organizational commitment.

In his book *Shine: Using Brain Science to Get the Best from Your People*, Edward Hallowell frames it this way: "I've learned that all people want to work hard and will work hard, given the right job and the right conditions, because it feels supremely good to excel....Great managers make this happen....You cannot do it with a stick, no matter how big a stick you wield. Nor can you do it with just a carrot, no matter how juicy the carrot....You must match the right people with the right jobs and environments. Craft the right setting, the proper culture, and the prime conditions under which people will *naturally* deliver their best, as naturally as a flower turns toward the sun and grows."

Like their counterparts in business and industry, many early childhood administrators believe that what their employees want most from their jobs are extrinsic rewards such as good wages, job security, and good working conditions. While these factors are important in reducing dissatisfaction, the research has consistently shown that workers rank intrinsic rewards, like the opportunity to learn new skills, recognition for a job well done, and participation in decisions that directly affect them, as more important in contributing to their job satisfaction.

So you see, this book is not about how to *make* people do what you want them to do, because no one can make someone do something they don't want to do. Instead it is a clarion call to examine how you currently structure supervision, professional development, and performance appraisal activities at your program and to think about ways those activities might be differentiated to more fully meet the unique needs, interests, and talents of each member on your team.

Supporting Individual and Organizational Change

Sounds like another cliché, but change in early childhood programs can come about only through change in individuals. There is no magic wand that can be waved to automatically create an exemplary program. Even if directors' financial woes evaporated overnight, it would not guarantee program excellence. The only way to achieve that distinction is through the hard work of engaging staff, one by one, in continuous quality improvement.

When we think of organizational change, we can view a professional learning community as both a goal—something we hope to achieve as the result of our change efforts—and a process—the action of implementing focused strategies to strengthen the competence, commitment, and collaborative capacity of everyone who works in the center. It happens one day at a time, person by person.

The harsh reality is that not all changes are successful. In fact, you've probably experienced firsthand some well-intentioned change efforts that ended up doing more harm than good. Maybe they resulted in putting the center at risk because funding stopped or enrollment dried up; maybe they created contentious collegial relations or underscored serious differences in core values and beliefs about what constitutes best practice. Let's look at four areas where a shift in thinking may be necessary to ensure that change is implemented in healthy and constructive ways.

If we don't change, we don't grow. If we don't grow, we aren't really living.

Gail Sheehy

19

A shift from trying to "fix" people (to correct their deficits) to building their strengths, interests, and natural talents. Our cultural fixation with weakness is deeply rooted in virtually every segment of our society. At all levels of our education system we tend to focus on remediating deficits in people rather than identifying and building on their strengths. An emerging body of research provides compelling evidence that this approach is simply wrong. The unrelenting focus on shoring up weaknesses saps people's motivation, stunts the creative process, and reduces the collective capacity of an organization to shine.

Leading the charge in this new way of thinking is the Gallup organization's Marcus Buckingham, author of the bestseller *Go Put Your Strengths to Work*. In his research with a wide variety of organizations, Buckingham has shown that it is a myth to think that people will grow most in their areas of greatest weakness. To the contrary, people are most inquisitive, resilient, creative, and open to learning in their areas of strength. Buckingham defines *strengths* as those specific activities at which a person does exceptionally well and retains a powerful appetite—in other words, the activities we do that just don't seem like work in the traditional sense of the word. Sadly, he found that only 17% of people report they are in jobs where they spend most of their time playing to their strengths.

This doesn't mean that we ignore those areas identified as weaknesses, but rather that we work to help people shape their jobs so that they use their strengths more. We include people in team projects that use their strengths and we structure opportunities for them to share their strengths with others. Buckingham is pretty emphatic in his conclusion: a person or an organization will excel only by amplifying strengths, never by simply fixing weaknesses. He states, "While there are many good levers for engaging people and driving performance—selecting for talent, setting clear expectations, praising where praise is due, and defining the team's mission—the *master lever* is getting each person to play to his strengths."

A shift from implementing bold, sweeping changes to making small, incremental improvements. We live in a quick-fix culture where bold innovations and sweeping changes are the name of the game. Many of the educational reform initiatives implemented over the past decade seem to fall into this category. But the change literature has shown that these ambitious attempts to jump-start transformational change often fail or end up producing disappointing results.

Instead, a more thoughtful, systematic way to support individual change (and thus organizational change) is to help people think of creative ways they can refine and do their jobs better, taking on small, doable improvements. The Japanese use the term *kaizen* to describe how small, incremental steps can often lead to bold change. This approach has a far higher success rate because it is more likely that people's interest and commitment will remain high when they see small tangible evidence of progress toward their goals.

A shift from viewing teaching as an isolated classroom enterprise to a centerwide, collegial endeavor. Because early childhood teachers often work in classroom teams of two or three, they tend to be more collaborative than teachers in elementary or secondary settings who have distinct silos of practice. Even so, at the early childhood level there is often little collaboration across classrooms. If it does exist, the collaboration typically focuses on a specific activity or project like planning a back-to-school event or family fun fair.

A professional learning community extends this spirit of collaboration one step further. It advances teachers beyond planning for events or organized projects to sustained opportunities to meet together to reflect on children's learning, plan curricula, tackle tough issues, and help each other reflect on and strengthen pedagogical practice. The goal is to help people move from being responsible for just their own learning to developing a collective responsibility for each other's learning.

Parker Palmer cautions that these shifts in thinking and in practice do not come easily. When people typically come together in schools, he says, they are "filled with the fear of being judged because we are in the business of fixing, saving, advising, and setting each other straight." It takes time to build trusting relationships where teachers can provide thoughtful feedback and support for one another.

In cultures of collaborative practice, the focus and core value is clear— the co-construction of a shared knowledge base. Teachers share strategies and professional resources, and they engage in systematic and ongoing experimentation to learn from and with their colleagues.

A shift from using data solely for accountability purposes to using data as a tool to support continuous quality improvement. In an era of early learning standards and state quality rating and improvement systems, directors have become accustomed to the new reality of the accountability movement. The drive to ensure regulatory compliance coupled with the push to document child outcomes has created an endless stream of assessments, paperwork, and forms to fill out. Most directors look upon these activities as a necessary evil to maintain their funding and document program effectiveness. They collect the data they are required to collect and ship it off to the appropriate monitoring agency. Job done!

While there seems to be an abundance of data, few directors and teachers know how to use the data to develop and implement quality improvement plans and then to benchmark progress in achieving their individual and organizational goals. What we have is a missed opportunity.

A report issued by the National Center on Quality Teaching and Learning calls for program directors to be evidence-based leaders—individuals who are "committed to implementing effective data collection systems to evaluate not only child and family outcomes but also the professional growth and development of program staff." Evidence-based leaders, the report goes on to say, "know the appropriate information to collect, how to analyze it, how to apply it to make positive program changes, how to use it to galvanize staff, and how to communicate it to their boards and extended community." We would add that this is not a leadership skill that should be reserved for directors, but one that should be held by many at the center.

The Organizational Context

It is often said that context is everything. And how true this is when it comes to your role in navigating the currents of change to achieve a program of excellence. Organizational context matters because it shapes the supportive (or constraining) factors that will determine your success in applying the concepts and strategies detailed in this book. The basic needs of staff and the components of good supervision, professional development, and performance appraisal do not change with the setting, but the organizational context certainly impacts how these practices are carried out.

The organizational context includes such things as program size, administrative structure, funding level, regulatory requirements, and the human and technical resources the program can draw on. The population served by your program also

Collecting data is not the same as using data.

Frederick Hess

has a profound impact on so many of the factors relating to how your center meets its mandate for supporting children and families. For example, if your program serves a large number of low-income families, dual language learners, or children with special needs, how you use data or structure professional development supports for your teachers will vary.

Some of these contextual factors you may have control over; others may be set in stone, given the funding source, location, and history of your center. For example, if your program is part of a larger agency that mandates certain practices counter to your management philosophy, you will feel thwarted in your efforts. The point is that your desire to create a professional learning community and inspire peak performance doesn't happen in a vacuum. The key is to be aware of the unique organizational context in which you work so that you can modify those factors that are in your control and begin to advocate for changing those factors that are not in your control.

Let's take a look at one aspect of organizational context—program size—to see how it affects your role as director in supporting your staff.

Small programs. In small programs (those with fewer than 10 staff), the director often plays a dual role, serving as a teacher for part of the day and attending to administrative tasks the rest of the time. In small programs the responsibility of orienting new staff, providing supervision, coordinating staff development, and conducting performance evaluations usually falls squarely on the director's shoulders. It is no wonder that directors of small programs talk about the tremendous workload they bear and the stress of juggling so many disparate responsibilities.

On the positive side, directors of small programs filling this dual role are literally on the floor every day working with children, connecting with families, and talking with other teachers. They have grounded, firsthand knowledge of how things are going. They are in the action every day, supporting less experienced teachers and modeling best practices. And they have a wealth of knowledge with which to evaluate teachers' performance.

The reality of managing a small program is that small usually means fewer financial resources to tap for professional development. Small programs may also have less flexibility in their staffing patterns and greater vulnerability when change occurs. If a beloved teacher leaves a large program, a director can usually shift staffing assignments until a new teacher can be found. In a small program, the departure of one superstar teacher can have an immediate consequence on the stability of enrollment, and thus on the program's reputation.

Medium-size programs. In medium-size programs (those with 10 to 30 staff), the director may work with an assistant director or education coordinator in providing pedagogical leadership and administrative oversight for the program. Medium-size programs may also have staffing configurations where lead teachers have some supervisory responsibility. With several people providing supervision, coordinating professional development, and conducting performance evaluations, the pressure of having to "do it all" that small-program directors feel is gone. It also means the director has someone else with a big-picture perspective to bounce ideas off.

The challenge for directors of medium-size programs comes with the increased necessity to coordinate the many activities going on in the center and communicating expectations for those activities. As the program size increases, the need for effective systems to ensure timeliness, consistency, and quality also increases.

In general, as program size increases so too does the distance of the director to the day-to-day action in the classroom. This creates an uncomfortable pull for some directors. It is why some centers have moved to a shared services model where administrative tasks such as budget, recruiting staff, and food management are outsourced to another agency. The goal of shared-services models is to free up time for directors to serve as pedagogical leaders and focus more on curriculum and supervision.

Large programs. In large programs (those with more than 30 staff), the director may work with a leadership team and a host of other professional staff sharing responsibility for teacher induction, ongoing supervision, staff development, and performance appraisal. The exciting part of leading a large program is that there are usually greater resources to support different staffing patterns, differentiated professional development, and one-on-one mentoring of staff who may need extra help.

On the flip side, the larger the program, the greater the range of opinions the director encounters on any particular issue. Coalescing support for a unified vision requires not only effective interpersonal skills and being savvy in managing the group dynamic, but also a commitment to shared decision making and the ability to structure conversations and stimulate dialog that mobilizes change.

Large programs without well-established systems in place are a recipe for chaos. While small- and medium-size programs can get by with rudimentary systems for the implementation of policies and procedures, large programs, by virtue of the increased number of staff and children involved, need well-oiled systems to ensure the program's smooth functioning.

Take time now to think about the unique organizational context of your program as you complete Exercise 3.

The organizational context of every center is different. Jot down some notes about your program in response to the following questions.

- How does the size of your program impact your role? In other words, what do you spend your time on each day?

- How have changes in federal, state, or local regulations affected your center in recent years?

- If your program is part of a larger agency or affiliated with a company, school district, or faith-based organization, how does that affiliation affect your ability to make decisions about your staff?

- If you report to a governing board or an independent owner of the center, how does that reporting relationship influence your ability to make decisions about your staff?

- Are your center's systems effective in communicating information internally and externally?

- How does the geographic location of the center impact your ability to marshal the financial, technological, and professional development resources you need to inspire peak performance?

- Are the current supervisory relationships effective in supporting teachers' ongoing professional development?

CHAPTER 3

Developmental Supervision: The Foundation for Reflective Practice

Imagine building meaningful relationships with your teachers that go beyond casual morning greetings and periodic classroom check-ins—relationships where you connect and support their learning and growth with intention. In the same way that a skilled teacher builds on each child's developmental level and interests, you play a parallel role in facilitating teachers' growth based on their unique interests, strengths, and level of competency—a trusting relationship that provides focused one-on-one support for strengthening professional practice.

The goal of developmental supervision is straightforward—to help teachers deepen their knowledge and embrace needed changes while also trusting them to find their own voice and develop skills in an autonomous way. The desired outcome of this process is also straightforward—to help teachers become more intentional in the way they engage children and extend their learning. In this book our examples focus on your supervisory relationship with classroom teachers, but this approach is also applicable to professional and support staff who fill other roles in your program.

Just who on your team assumes the role of supervisor for your teachers depends on your organizational context. In small programs, as we noted in the previous chapter, supervision may be your sole responsibility. In medium-size or larger programs, it may be carried out by an assistant director or even a lead teacher assigned to an age-group team. Regardless of who assumes the role, the essential principles of the model are the same.

In this chapter we first explore the core features of developmental supervision and the importance of establishing a relationship-based approach built on trust, mutual respect, and confidentiality. Next, we zero in on the importance of attentive listening and how we can nurture teachers' dispositions to be reflective practitioners constructing knowledge and insight from the inside out. Finally, we address the essential supervisory skill of asking good questions to support authentic learning conversations.

Flexing Your Supervisory Style

Developmental supervision rests on the assumption that teachers are unique learners with differing needs and expectations and in various stages of adult growth and development. These differences relate to variables such as cognitive, conceptual, moral, and ego development. Teachers' levels of abstract thinking, for example, can influence their receptivity to different supervisory strategies and their overall level of performance in the classroom.

Developmental supervision provides differential support for teachers in different phases of the adult life cycle, capitalizing on young teachers' excitement and idealism, supporting middle-age teachers as they reprioritize goals, and providing opportunities for veteran teachers to consolidate achievement and transition to retirement. Additionally, it structures supervisory supports according to teachers' concerns at different stages of their careers—survival, consolidation, renewal, maturity—providing individual supports along the way.

Developmental Stages of Teacher's Concerns

Stage	Concerns
Maturity	Finding new perspectives and insight Sharing knowledge and experience
Renewal	Sustaining enthusiasm Maintaining interest in new developments
Consolidation	Handling individual problem children Solving problem situations
Survival	Surviving in the job Being accepted by colleagues

From Katz, L. (1972). Developmental stages of preschool teachers. *Elementary School Journal, 73*, 50–55.

Developmental supervision underscores the importance of helping teachers navigate and learn from different life transition events, balance the demands of personal and professional roles, and engage in identifying and solving their own concerns and problems. Such involvement helps deepen awareness of the impact of different courses of action and empowers teachers by focusing on their strengths and their insights into their own thinking processes. A developmental approach also considers the sociocultural context of the teacher and how gender, race, ethnicity, class, and ability may impact their professional identity, preferences, and learning goals.

A developmental approach rests on the premise that individuals who function at different conceptual levels, who are at different stages of their careers, and who show different levels of commitment to the profession should be supervised in qualitatively different ways. For example, teachers who are more concrete in their conceptualization or are in their first year of teaching usually benefit from a more structured supervisory approach. Capable and mature teachers who function at a high level of conceptualization and demonstrate a strong commitment to their work need a less structured approach.

In order to move teachers forward in their thinking, a supervisor needs to begin where each teacher functions by presenting ideas and opportunities that meet the teacher's identified developmental level. Sound familiar? This process parallels the developmental approach we advocate for young children. Lev Vygotsky's *zone of proximal development* is a concept just as applicable to adults as it is to children. Vygotsky believed that development should not be viewed as a fixed entity, but rather as a dynamic and constantly changing continuum of behavior. Your role as supervisor, then, is one of assisting, or scaffolding, the teacher to higher levels of conceptual thinking and behavior.

Carl Glickman, a thought leader in the area of instructional leadership, provides a useful framework for thinking about supervisory styles that relate to the issue of control and responsibility. A *directive* style is characterized by high supervisor control and low teacher control. In a *collaborative* style responsibility is conceptualized more equally. A supervisory relationship built on low supervisor control and high teacher control is referred to as a *nondirective* style. According to Glickman, all three approaches are valid as long as they are linked to the developmental needs of teachers and aim to increase teachers' responsibility. The following continuum captures these three approaches.

The art of supervision is the art of assisting discovery.

Mark VanDoren

Supervisory Behavior Continuum

Directive	Collaborative	Nondirective
→	→	→
High supervisor control Low teacher control		High teacher control Low supervisor control

When teachers are unskilled, unmotivated, or very new to the profession, a directive style may be the best approach. The goal with these teachers is to provide the structure and information they need to strengthen their level of competency and capacity for self-reflection. We'll talk more about the special case of new teachers in the next chapter.

When teachers have had some experience, have shown success and competency, and appear motivated, collaborative strategies are more successful. The collaborative style encourages a frank exchange of ideas and differences of opinion. The supervisory relationship is viewed as a partnership, and there is equality in problem-solving exchanges.

For teachers who have extensive experience, have demonstrated independence and autonomy, and have high problem-solving abilities, a nondirective style is most appropriate. A nondirective style is based on the assumption that a teacher knows best what changes need to be made and has the ability to think and act on his or her own. The role of the supervisor is to assist the teacher in thinking through different courses of action.

Developmental supervision isn't about providing a quick fix, correcting mistakes, finding fault, or assessing blame. Rather, it's about making deep human connections that personalize the supervisory experience, allowing the teacher to reduce reliance on the supervisor as expert and instead become a valued partner in learning. Exercise 4 provides an opportunity for you to apply some of the developmental supervision concepts to your specific work context.

Think about one teacher who works at your center. Using the table on page 17, "Some of the Ways Individuals Differ," list the many characteristics and attributes that make this person unique. Describe the person in as much detail as you can.

_____

_____

_____

_____

_____

_____

_____

_____

_____

_____

Now, drawing on your understanding of the person's strengths, commitment to the field, conceptual level, and career stage, think about which supervisory style might be most appropriate to use with this individual—directive, collaborative, or nondirective.

_____

_____

_____

Trusting Relationships—The Heart of Effective Supervision

One-on-one trusting relationships are at the heart of effective supervision. While both the supervisor and the teacher play an essential role in creating and sustaining an interpersonal dynamic characterized by openness, honesty, and mutual respect, it is the supervisor who sets the tone from the first interaction. This is because in all supervisor–employee relationships there is a power dynamic at play. As a supervisor, you need to be comfortable talking about that power dynamic.

When supervising teachers, you want to create a climate built on trust that encourages teachers to ask for help, share the issues and challenges they are experiencing, and discuss their areas of uncertainty and insecurity. The tricky part is that if you also serve as the evaluator of their performance, making decisions about merit increases or contract renewal, that power over others may inhibit their willingness to ask for help and expose any feelings of inadequacy. The tension between these twin roles—*supervisor* and *evaluator*—becomes a problem only if the roles are viewed as discrete functions rather than part of a unified system of individual and organizational improvement.

The key is to be open about these dual responsibilities right from the start. Help the teacher understand that you both have a responsibility to help create a program of excellence and at the same time create a workplace in which individuals experience personal and professional fulfillment. This helps move the relationship from a hierarchical one (having power over another) to a mutually supportive collegial one (sharing power with another).

At a primal level every teacher has a basic need—to know that you care about him or her as a person. There is no shortcut here. Investing time (yes, substantial time) right from the beginning of your relationship to learn a teacher's life story is essential. Even if you've worked with the person previously as a colleague, but not in a supervisory capacity, taking the time to talk about his or her professional journey is crucial. In your initial conversations it is important to talk about the person's previous work experiences. How was he or she supervised in the past? What went well in that supervisory relationship, and what didn't go so well?

Talking openly about the teacher's and your expectations for the supervisory relationship is essential. This lays the foundation for aligning your supervisory goals. Understanding their point of view—their perspective on different issues— will strengthen your relationship.

It is a myth that supervision can be a totally objective process. Caruso and Fawcett remind us that supervision is a complex activity, and all supervisors come to the role with "colored glasses." The way you view your teachers is

> P eople don't care how much you know until they know how much you care.
>
> *John Maxwell*

affected by your own childhood, education, life, and work experiences and the philosophy and values you have developed. Your beliefs and values cannot be set aside, but they should be recognized.

As you talk with your teachers, reflect on your tendency to filter what they say through your own value lens. Be brutally honest with yourself: What are your assumptions? What are your biases? What ticks you off? Why are you so quick to jump on some transgressions and gloss over others? Your personal reflections are essential for strengthening your own supervisory capacity.

There are also many cross-cultural nuances in relationships that have an impact on our ability to build trust and establish rapport. Being aware of the cultural background and communication expectations of the other person helps you navigate this sometimes confusing terrain and avoid inadvertently offending the other person.

We've all made mistakes in this area. Even Bill Gates was criticized when he greeted the president of South Korea during a summit of global leaders, extending his right hand for a handshake but leaving his left hand in his pocket. This, it turns out, is a serious no-no in international protocol. Your gaffes probably won't make the evening news, but still you want to make sure you attend to the small things that can undermine rapport.

Characteristics of Good Supervisors

Good supervisors are...

- **positive**—focusing energy on what's good and what works.
- **curious**—asking open-ended questions and eagerly exploring possibilities.
- **specific and focused**—dealing in particulars and keeping tasks manageable.
- **respectful**—treating teachers as valued colleagues.
- **observant**—keeping their eyes and ears open, tuning in to what isn't said as well as what is.
- **patient**—understanding that change takes time.
- **compassionate**—expressing empathy and concern for teachers' challenging moments.
- **open**—willing to share their own professional journey, strengths, and vulnerabilities.

Attentive Listening Is Not a Passive Activity

On self-assessments, directors often equate their ability to be good supervisors with the number of management courses they've taken, their years of experience, or how many coaching books they have stacked on their bookshelf. But the truth is, the most powerful tool you have in your supervision toolbox is your ability to be an attentive listener. While human connections are never simple, one thing is certain, they can't happen without good listening skills. Make no mistake about it, attentive listening is not a passive activity.

Good listening skills are at the core of building the trusting relations that inspire peak performance. Attentive listening means being fully engaged and suppressing the desire to interrupt, speed up the discussion, or share your own life story. It means structuring the time so that you are not rushed, and finding a place to meet that minimizes the possibility of interruptions. It also means making sure that your cell phone is off and eliminating any other distractions that prevent you from being fully present.

Parker Palmer writes about the powerful connection between good listening and "honoring the human heart." He says, "Our society teaches us to try to fix each other, to judge, to find fault. If you come to me with a problem, I'll listen to you for about three minutes and then give you my advice. I'll tell you what I would do if I were in your shoes or suggest that you read a particular book or attend some workshop. This way of relating to each other is deeply ingrained in us. But what the human heart really wants is not to be fixed, but to be heard and received."

Marshall Cook also talks about the connection to the heart when he makes the distinction between *head-centered* listening and *heart-centered* listening. In head-centered listening we tend to hear and absorb less than one-half of what the other person is saying. We are looking for ways to respond from our own viewpoint, like a conversational tennis match. Each statement the other person lobs at us, we come back with a similar response. There's a connection, but it's superficial. In heart-centered listening we slide out of our own worldview so we can learn more about the other speaker, asking thoughtful questions that open the door for a deeper connection. There is no judgment, no analysis, and no advice.

If you are interested in strengthening your capacity to be an attentive listener, take time to complete Exercise 5. This exercise comes from *Leadership in Action*, one of the other books in the Director's Toolbox Management series.

☐ I usually think about my response while the other person is talking.

☐ I am impatient with people who don't get right to the point.

☐ I often finish sentences for other people.

☐ I am too busy to engage in friendly chitchat.

☐ I carry on a conversation with someone while I am doing another task (sorting papers, organizing my desk, doodling).

☐ Sometimes I just "tune out" when the topic of conversation doesn't interest me.

☐ When I know what the other person is trying to say, I interrupt and respond.

☐ Sometimes I am so busy focusing on the details of what someone says that I miss their main point.

☐ I find it difficult to maintain eye contact while another person is talking, so I tend to look at other objects in the room.

☐ I am inclined to give answers and solutions when teachers approach me about issues.

☐ I feel uncomfortable when people express anger, hurt, discouragement, or hopelessness, so I try to say things that will make the feeling go away.

☐ I occasionally sneak a look at my watch while others are talking to me.

☐ I find myself debating issues with people rather than discussing them.

☐ I often interrupt a speaker to ask questions for clarification.

☐ I am uncomfortable with pauses during conversations.

A loving silence often has far more power to heal and to connect than the most well-intentioned words.

Rachel Remen

So what insights did you discover about yourself as you read through the items relating to these different listening behaviors? Are there some items you checked that you feel might be undermining the rapport you are trying to establish with your teachers? Consider the personal changes you might want to make in your listening style to enhance your ability to be a better supervisor. Attentive, focused listening is one of the most treasured gifts you can give your teachers.

Listening attentively also means being aware of your body language—eye contact, posture, facial expressions, gestures, and how your body is positioned in relation to the other person. Sitting behind a desk or even on the other side of a table can sometimes create an emotional distance between you and the other person.

And what about note taking? Because directors often supervise several teachers, some like to take brief notes so they can remember key issues or remind themselves about action steps they need to take. If your note taking makes the conversation feel like a press conference then clearly you are better off leaving your notepad in your desk drawer. But if your note taking communicates your genuine interest in what the teacher is saying, then by all means, it can be a good thing.

It's hard to talk about attentive listening without discussing the issue of silence. Most people feel uncomfortable with more than a nanosecond of silence in a conversation (make that really uncomfortable). How comfortable are you with pauses in the flow of conversation? Do you find yourself in a rush to fill the void? We know that in the classroom, when teachers are comfortable with more wait time after they ask questions to children, the quantity and quality of answers they get improves. Silence gives everyone more time to absorb what has been said and invites those who process information more deliberately a chance to respond. Give it a try. Experiment to see if increasing your wait time for a response changes the dynamic of your conversations with your teachers.

Nurturing Reflective Practice

Ever wonder why low-performing teachers don't voluntarily try to improve themselves? Kruger and Dunning, two researchers at the University of Illinois, have found that most incompetent people simply don't know they're incompetent. In fact, they discovered that in many cases, people who do things poorly actually appear more confident of their abilities than people who do things well. Directors cannot assume that teachers will be reflective, autonomous, and responsible for their own development. Directors need to be intentional in their efforts to nurture teachers' reflective practice.

We believe that the ability to reflect is a disposition that can be strengthened. We also believe teachers' capacity for reflective practice directly relates to their sense of job fulfillment and their ability to be effective in the classroom. In most centers, supervisory conversations with teachers tend to focus exclusively on curriculum content, instructional methods, and learning outcomes. These are obviously important discussion areas in any educational setting, but we can't forget teachers' inner lives, the soul of good practice.

Robert Kegan describes the subtle distinction using two contrasting terms— *informational learning* versus *transformational learning*. Informational learning focuses on what a person knows; it is technical in nature. Transformational learning focuses on how a person knows what he or she knows; it is adaptive in nature. Good supervision focuses on both aspects—moving individuals to higher levels of skills and knowledge (what they know) while altering the very thought processes by which they deepen their understanding of their professional practice (how they know).

Teachers long for supervisors who not only help them sharpen their knowledge and skills, but also help them think more deeply about their sense of purpose and, more broadly, about the purpose of early childhood education. If we help teachers to articulate their personal vision for who they want to be in the lives of the children and families, and then help them to regularly reflect on how they live that vision in their classroom practice, we go a long way toward keeping alive their sense of passion for teaching.

Deb Curtis, Margie Carter, and their colleagues at Harvest Resources have been passionate proponents of helping teachers learn to use a reflective lens as a key component of responsive, child-centered teaching. In their book *Reflecting in Communities of Practice*, they state, "Because each child and each teaching situation is unique, effective teachers must continuously reflect on their reactions to everything that happens in the classroom.... Rather than just following preplanned lessons and techniques, reflective teachers consider what they know about the children in their group and about child development theory to better understand and delight in what happens in the classroom."

If you are interested in deepening your understanding about the power of reflective practice, we encourage you to read *From the Inside Out*, another volume in the Director's Toolbox management series. That book identifies three different types of reflection. The most common is *reflection-on-action*. This is simply a replay of an experience in order to review, revisit, or recall what happened, like replaying a videotape. *Reflection-in-action* refers to a kind of out-of-body experience in which we watch ourselves act and simultaneously reflect about the

While no conversation is guaranteed to change the trajectory of a career, a company, a relationship, or a life— any single conversation can.

Susan Scott

decisions we are making. A third type of reflection is referred to as *reflection-for-action*. This is a predictive process for forecasting how we will use what we have learned from reflection-in-action and reflection-on-action. It involves consciously adjusting our behaviors based on our reflections.

The content or substance of reflection also goes through a change as teachers gain mastery in their work. As they strengthen their capacity for critical reflection, they are better able to recognize the gap between their *espoused theories* (what they say) and their *theories-in-action* (what they actually do). Later on in this chapter we share some question-asking strategies that can help teachers bridge this gap.

So how do you nurture the disposition for reflective practice? First, you focus on teachers' inner lives to tap their core beliefs about the purpose of education and the qualities of exemplary teachers: Why do they do this work? What are their hopes and dreams for children? What do they find most satisfying and most frustrating about teaching?

Second, you shift the focus from what teachers do (teaching) to the children's experiences in the classroom and what they are learning. This helps teachers move from an *input* perspective (what they are doing) to an *output* perspective (what the children are experiencing and learning). This sounds like jargon, but sometimes this simple shift in focus helps make teachers less defensive and begin to more critically examine the consequences of their actions.

From a developmental perspective, you'll find your teachers have differing levels of ability in being able to reflect on their professional practice. You may even encounter a wall of silence with some teachers who have a low capacity for inner reflection. You'll need to tailor your strategies accordingly. Patience is essential. At first, teachers will rely on you as the source of wisdom and advice; but as your relationships become grounded and their reflective capacities increase, you'll be able to step back from the role of expert, providing advice and direction, and become instead a valued colleague, helping them to reflect, explore, analyze, and dig deeper into the essence of good practice.

Remember, how you frame the art and science of teaching has everything to do with how your teachers view the important work they do. Ann Pelo says that early childhood programs ought to be "incubators of inquiry where children, teachers, families, and program administrators collectively and individually engage in systematic investigation, searching and researching, asking questions, mulling over hypotheses, debating, trying on new perspectives." If you're looking for a succinct vision for your program, there it is! And it all begins by nurturing that disposition for reflective practice.

The Power of Good Questions

Our days are full of questions. Some questions we ask; others we answer. Some are routine, extracting ordinary information we need to carry out everyday activities; others are thought-provoking, making us ponder the deeper meaning of our existence. Some questions make us laugh, strengthening our bond with friends; others are offensive, driving a wedge between us. Good questions are at the heart of effective supervision and essential for nurturing teachers' reflective practice.

Not all questions are created equal, though. Learning how to formulate good questions is a leadership skill that takes practice. The first step is to analyze your own question-asking behavior, recognizing when you are asking *closed-ended* versus *open-ended* questions.

Closed-ended questions are straightforward, simple requests that ask for information, facts, or details. They help clarify the topic or the issue being discussed. Closed-ended questions are investigative in nature. They can be answered with a simple yes or no or a very brief answer. Closed questions are appropriate when there are specific facts that need to be gathered.

- "Did you turn in the receipts for the classroom supplies you purchased?"
- "How long did the children nap today?"
- "Did Rachel's mother sign her field trip permission slip?"

Open-ended questions, on the other hand, help increase awareness and understanding. They are designed to prompt a deeper level of reflection, drawing out a teacher's ideas and feelings about different issues. Open-ended questions are more empowering because they stimulate more complex responses about a person's opinions, thoughts, or feelings. They can't be answered with a yes or no and usually begin with "What" or "How."

- "What do you think about the grouping arrangement?"
- "How would you like to handle the situation with Jason's mother?"

Many of the issues that teachers confront have no easy answers. Sharp, incisive questions can help teachers discover their own answers and unleash their creative energy to envision new possibilities. In a nutshell, good questions help support teachers' continued growth and success.

The key, from a supervisory standpoint, is to frame questions so that the exchange doesn't seem like an interrogation. For this reason it is important to avoid asking "Why" questions whenever possible. Questions like, "Why was

Effective leaders motivate people not by the answers they give, but rather by the questions they ask.

Jeremy left alone in the nap room?" or "Why did you do that?" immediately put a teacher on the defensive. They imply that you have already made a judgment about their actions.

Instead, starting with a stem such as "I'm curious about how ..." or "Help me understand how ..." can lead to a more productive conversation to understand the rationale for behavior rather than the finger-pointing tone implied when using why.

In analyzing your questions, think also about the presuppositions they imply. Consider these two questions, both seeking to elicit information about the same thing:

- "Did you contribute to the meeting?"
- "In what ways did you contribute to the meeting's success?"

The first version is a far less useful inquiry than the second. Focused questions that presume positive intentionality help teachers become more thoughtful about their actions. They help avoid unintentional put-downs. They can also help shape expectations.

Different Types of Questions

Carefully constructed questions can serve many functions. They can keep information flowing, support reflection about beliefs and values, promote insight into others' perspectives, and expand awareness about different courses of action. Think of questions as the protein powder to fortify your supervisor–teacher relationships. Here are a few ways that questions can help teachers.

Questions that help teachers reflect on their professional practice

- "What was the most challenging part of the morning session for you?"
- "How did you feel when that happened?"
- "What do you think prompted Jacob's outburst?"
- "What aspect of the documentation panels are you most pleased with?"
- "What classroom situation did you find most puzzling this week?"
- "How do you feel about the way your recycling project is going so far?"

Questions that help teachers define a problem, evaluate options, and make a decision

- "How do you feel about the current situation?"

- "What factors may have contributed to this situation?"

- "What do you think will happen if things continue the way they are now?"

- "What's the most important thing you'd like to see happen?"

- "If the situation changed in the way you'd like it to, how would it impact what you do?"

- "What are your options in this situation?"

- "What else do you need to know in order to make a good decision about this?"

- "Who else should we consult with before making a decision?"

Questions that help teachers consider different perspectives

- "Who might have a different opinion on this issue?"

- "When Monica's mom said you weren't meeting her expectations, what do you think she meant?"

- "How do you think the parents will react to the biting incident?"

- "How will this decision impact the teachers in the toddler room?"

- "How will other people be affected by this change?"

Questions that help teachers connect the past and present with the future

- "How does this decision support the goals you shared the last time we met?"

- "What have you learned from this experience that will help when we revise our parent handbook?"

- "When you faced a similar situation like this in the past, what did you learn that will help you deal with this one?"

Questions that help teachers clarify or expand their thinking

- "Can you give me an example for that?"

- "Let me see if I understand your position. Are you saying that ...?"

- "When you said the children were 'out of control,' what exactly did you mean?"

Different Types of Questions (continued)

Questions that help teachers identify and express their wants or needs

- "What kind of support do you need to ensure success in using this new assessment?"

- "What are two specific things I could do to help you move this along?"

- "What is your biggest fear about working with a challenging child like Ryan?"

- "What kind of support do you need from your co-teachers to help you deal with this situation?"

- "What concerns do you have as we move to a new performance appraisal process?"

Questions that help teachers connect what they are doing with the center's mission

- "What are some of the ways that your 'Meet the Author' project supports the center's literacy goals?"

- "How do you describe the center's mission in your conversations with parents?"

- "Was there anything you learned at the workshop that could benefit other staff?"

Questions to help teachers pinpoint what is going well and reaffirm goals

- "What was the most rewarding part of the morning for you?"

- "What interaction with a child this week delighted you most?"

- "How did that activity support your learning goals with Anthony?"

- "What did you learn by observing Angela's classroom this morning that will help you deal with Roberto's challenging behavior in your classroom?"

While supervisory relationships are often complex and murky, and the interpersonal dynamics between supervisor and teacher are filled with highs and lows, the intended outcome of supervision is crystal clear—to empower, engage, and strengthen the professional competency of teachers. Supervisors provide the focus, structure, and time for one-on-one exchanges that create a positive path forward. When connections are strong and time for meeting regularly is honored, supervision can be an active force for reducing isolation, validating best practice, and strengthening teachers' capacities to think deeply about the important work they do with young children and families.

CHAPTER 4

Teacher Induction: A Lifeline for Novice Teachers

Imagine a work environment where there is dedicated time and attention to support teachers in the early stages of their careers— an environment where emerging professionals are nurtured and guided toward long-term success in early childhood education. Envision a process where you are able to capture the enthusiasm and idealism of new teachers and help them experience deep personal and professional fulfillment during their first year on the job.

The hard truth is that very few novice teachers step into jobs with this kind of supportive work environment. The more common scenario experienced by first-year teachers revolves around stories of disillusionment and dashed expectations. It is not uncommon to hear teachers reflecting on their first year of teaching using colorful language like "reality shock," "sink-or-swim," or "trial by fire." The attrition rate in the first few years is staggering, prompting some to call education "the profession that eats its young."

Both teacher turnover (where teachers leave their job but stay in the field) and teacher attrition (where teachers leave the field altogether) threaten the stability of our programs, affecting staff morale and compromising the essential adult–child relationships that are at the heart of our professional practice. And as you know all too well, every time a teacher leaves your program it impacts your center's bottom line, in both direct replacement costs and indirect costs related to your administrative workload.

It doesn't need to be this way. Other fields, like medicine and law, recognize the needs of new recruits and have implemented professional pathways that support the beginner. In early childhood education it is even more important that we address this issue because so many new teachers have limited specialized training in child development or early childhood instructional methods. Even those with two- or four-year degrees may have had limited opportunities to bridge theory and practice.

In early childhood education, teacher induction programs may hold the answer to retaining and developing promising and committed teachers. Induction programs recognize that the beginning teacher is not a finished product—even one who may have completed a teacher certification program. All first-year teachers take more time to do what experienced veterans consider routine teaching activities. And virtually all novice teachers experience moments of self-doubt and a sense of being overwhelmed by the physical and emotional demands of the job. It is our profession's collective responsibility to help beginning teachers by creating a more predictable and assured path to competence building.

While all new employees need a systematic introduction to a program's policies and practices, and socialization into the program's culture, novice teachers need much more. They need regularly scheduled opportunities to meet with you, their supervisor, or an assigned mentor with whom to reflect on practice, receive focused feedback, and chart incremental steps for skill building.

In *The Right Fit: Recruiting, Selecting, and Orienting Staff*, author Kay Albrecht lays out a phased approach for employee orientation. A teacher induction program includes similar components but differs in timing and intensity. Where a new employee orientation should take between one and three months to implement, a well-designed beginning teacher induction program should be at least a full year. In this chapter you'll see how Albrecht's phased approach to orientation can be used as a template for developing a more comprehensive and systematic teacher induction program for your center. First though, let's take a look at why beginning teachers need our focused attention.

Beginning Teachers Deserve Our Focused Support

The term *novice teacher* describes a variety of individuals who assume a teaching role in early childhood programs. Some enter teaching in their early twenties, fresh from a two- or four-year degree program. For them, their first "real" job coincides with the life transition events of young adulthood—living independently, buying a car, using a credit or debit card for the first time. On the outside they may be brimming with enthusiasm and excited about making a difference in the lives of children; on the inside they may be terrified at leaving the supportive cocoon of a college environment and good friends.

Young females, in particular, often worry they won't be taken seriously or have credibility with the parents of their students because they don't have children of their own. The great thing about young adults, though, is that they are ready to learn from you and the experienced teachers on your team. They are open and receptive to feedback during their first year on the job and eager to be viewed as true professionals.

Some beginning teachers are older and more mature. They may have extensive work experience, a degree in a related field, and perhaps children of their own. These older novices typically assume their new roles with more realistic expectations, but that doesn't mean they feel any more confident on the inside. In fact, older adults often harbor deep insecurities because they believe others expect them to be able to slide into their new roles with ease. Consequently, many are reluctant to ask for help for fear of looking inept.

Whether novice teachers are young or older adults, their first year of teaching provides an important opportunity for shaping their sense of identity and commitment to the field. During the first year, new teachers are more receptive to guidance and feedback than at any other point in their careers. The first year is so critical because it sets the tone and expectations for reflective practice, for ongoing professional development, and for collaborating with colleagues.

The demands during the first year of teaching are daunting. Most novice teachers struggle with classroom management issues and how to support children with special needs, particularly those who exhibit disruptive behavior. Many are overwhelmed by the recordkeeping and paperwork required for child assessment, accreditation, and other aspects of program accountability. Young teachers, in particular, say they feel woefully inept in dealing with parents.

Left on their own, novice teachers will focus on whatever works. And if what they try isn't successful, their attempts will be met with frustration and despair. There is simply no research that shows that teachers become more effective working in isolation. The fate of first-year teachers can't be left to chance. A systematic teacher induction program serves as a lifeline, helping to ensure new teachers get the emotional and technical support they need.

Planning a Teacher Induction Program

A teacher induction program is built on the premise that all beginning teachers want to succeed. A comprehensive and well-designed program can help novice teachers do more than just survive their first year on the job. Instead, it can help them thrive in their new role, experiencing the success that lays the foundation for a long-term career in early childhood education.

A well-designed teacher induction program ...

- provides a thorough orientation to the policies, practices, and expectations of the center.

- validates the knowledge, skills, and life experience the novice teacher brings to the situation.

- provides new opportunities for skill-building in incremental, doable doses.

- includes regular classroom observations of the teachers' teaching and the children's learning, coupled with meaningful feedback.

- helps novice teachers develop a personal style that reflects their values, hopes, and aspirations in working with young children.

- provides the emotional support needed to navigate the ups and downs characteristic of the first year in a classroom.

- socializes the novice teacher into the life and culture of the center.

- cultivates the disposition for reflective practice and lifelong learning.

Now that you have a good understanding of the reason for implementing a systematic beginning-teacher induction program, let's take a look at how that program might play out. The plan we share in this chapter is designed to take place over twelve months. It includes three phases. The first phase, during a new teacher's first month of employment, focuses on making connections and building rapport. The second phase, learning the ropes, takes place over the next five months. This phase socializes the teacher into the culture of the center and includes an overview of all components of the teacher's job, including curriculum, assessment, and family relations. The final phase, skill building, covers the second half of the year. It focuses on deepening the teacher's understanding of best practice and reinforces norms of job-embedded professional development.

Just how you configure the induction experience for your novice teachers depends on each new teacher's level of knowledge and skill, the requirements of the specific position, and your center's supervisory structure. In small programs, the bulk of the work may fall on your shoulders, with help perhaps from a seasoned teacher. If you have a large program with assigned age-level team leaders who serve as supervisors, or an assistant director, education coordinator, or veteran teachers who can help mentor new staff, then your teacher induction program will include a larger team of people.

The induction plan needs to be tailored according to the type of program you administer and your center's annual calendar. Programs that provide full-day, full-year services, for example, may have new staff beginning at different points throughout the year. Sometimes directors of these programs can anticipate a new opening and plan an orderly transition from one teacher to the next; other times, teachers leave abruptly and there is pressure to get the new teacher up and running as quickly as possible. If the new teacher is also a first-year teacher, this can be challenging. If the program is a part-year program, with new teachers starting at the beginning of the new academic year, then your induction plan for a new first-year teacher might begin even before the children arrive for the first day of school. If your program is a part-day program, you may have additional flexibility for how you implement your beginning-teacher induction program.

Phase 1: Making Connections and Building Rapport

The first phase of induction covers the first month of a new teacher's employment contract and has two goals. The first goal is to ensure that the teacher becomes acquainted with the essential requirements and expectations of the position and completes the necessary human resources paperwork required of all new employees. The second goal is for the teacher to begin building rapport with an assigned supervisor and any other individuals who will be part of the yearlong induction process.

How we greet and welcome new teachers sets the stage for a mutually respectful work relationship. Just as a good teacher plans special experiences to welcome young children into a new classroom, you plan how to welcome new teachers to your center. This can begin before they officially report for work—a welcoming e-mail or letter sent to their home, along with a picture of their new colleagues and some helpful resources for their new job. A card, banner, or small bouquet on their first day also reinforces the message that your center is a special work environment. A new teacher's first few days will include the same activities that all new employees receive:

- A tour of the center to familiarize new teachers with the physical layout of the facility, including bathrooms, staff lounge, storage facilities, and storage for personal belongings

- Conversations with human resources staff and completion of paperwork related to payroll, insurance, retirement or other benefits, and leave policies

- Personal introductions to each staff member

- Introductions to essential job requirements, like first aid and rescue breathing requirements, and health and safety requirements, like TB testing, annual physicals, location of fire extinguishers, and operating entry systems

- Review of the center's mission and vision, educational philosophy, and values statements, followed by discussions with you and the new teacher's supervisor

- Review of work schedules, lunch and break policies, professional dress, and other personnel policies and procedures

- Creation of biographies for the center's newsletter or bio board for display outside the new teacher's classroom as an introduction to parents and visitors

While a gradual transition into assigned responsibilities is important for all new employees, it is ideal to adjust your staffing so you don't count first-year teachers in your required ratios for the first month. Structure this time to help them get acquainted with their colleagues, gain a clear understanding of their job responsibilities, and see where they fit into the larger picture.

Allowing time during the first month on the job for lengthy observations in each classroom will help novice teachers form new connections, see your center's educational philosophy in action, and learn how each colleague can serve as a resource during the years ahead. This is the time to encourage new teachers to ask lots of questions and for you to reinforce the idea with your entire team that every teacher has an important role to play in the center's teacher induction program. This will strengthen the program's norms of collaboration.

From a supervisory standpoint, the first month should be devoted to rapport building and assessing the needs of the new teacher. As we discussed in Chapter 3, establishing trust and open, honest, and authentic relationships is not something that can be rushed. This is the opportunity for you to build on the information you learned about the teachers during their job interview.

Curiosity is the best way to get the conversations started. You might ask them to share something about their name—how they were named, the cultural tradition or family folklore associated with their name, the spelling of their name, how they acquired a nickname, or what their name means to them personally. Here are some additional questions you can weave into your initial supervisory conversations:

- How did you get into the field?
- What are your special talents and interests?
- How would you define your core values: the things you feel most passionate about?

- What gets you excited? What makes you annoyed?
- What do you perceive as your strengths?
- What talents would you like to develop further?
- When do you feel most capable, engaged, and confident?
- What achievements are you most proud of?
- What traits do you admire most in other people?
- What are the important lessons you've learned from your parents or grandparents?

Also, don't be afraid to explore topics relating to their personal lives. What do they like to do in their free time? Are they involved in any civic or faith-based organizations? Do they have a favorite sports team? Helping beginning teachers learn to balance their work and their personal lives so they keep renewed personally and professionally is important during the first year.

By the end of Phase 1 of induction, new teachers should have a clear understanding of their job responsibilities as well as the most important skills and dispositions that define exemplary teaching. They should have a general understanding of the center's core values, expectations for their professional development, and how they will be evaluated during their first year.

As you wind up Phase 1, it is important to communicate that the induction process is a two-way learning experience. Here are a few questions that will help you solicit feedback about how the first month went:

- Were you made to feel welcome on your first day on the job? Did other staff know you were coming?
- Were you given the information you needed about the particulars of the center (parking, supplies, storage, lunch routines, schedules, etc.) to help you get though those first days?
- Were you given sufficient background on the center's policies, goals, and philosophy?
- Were you made to feel that others had a personal interest in your progress? Have other teachers made you feel like you are part of the team?
- Are there any policies or procedures you would like to know more about?

This semi-structured meeting to wrap up the first phase of induction will serve as a precursor to the center's performance appraisal process in which two-way communication about organizational functioning is the centerpiece for accountability and continuous quality improvement.

New teachers long for opportunities to learn from their experienced colleagues and want more than social support and instructions for using the copy machine.

Sharon Feiman-Nemser

Phase 2: Learning the Ropes

During the first phase of induction, beginning teachers receive an introduction to the critical pieces of information they need to function in their respective roles, and a broad view of the center, its culture, vision, and values. Phase 2 is about "learning the ropes" and being able to function independently or as part of a teaching team in the classroom. It is also the time for you to share more detailed information about the center—its history, funders, board of directors, short- and long-term goals, curriculum, policies, traditions and rituals, and accreditation.

From a developmental supervision perspective, the typical beginning teacher needs a fairly directive approach during Phase 2, with the primary responsibility for identifying appropriate supports resting with the supervisor. The purpose is to gradually move the teacher to a collaborative supervisory style by the end of Phase 2, with more equal distribution of responsibility between the supervisor and the teacher for identifying needs and resources for sharpening practice.

The goal of Phase 2 is to help the beginning teacher put into practice the educational priorities that shape decision making at your center. The transition from learning information to using it thoughtfully and intentionally is an important step in competence building. When this transition is successful, a new teacher understands not only your program's educational philosophy and how it is implemented, but also how that information informs his or her classroom teaching practices. Making this transition is not easy, so your role as supervisor is crucial.

Plan on two hours each week to work with a beginning teacher during Phase 2. This includes time for daily observations of practice, one-on-one meetings to go over the teacher's documentation of student learning, a review of assessment data, and discussions about articles, videos, or other resources you've identified as potentially helpful. The challenge during this phase is to structure new learning so it is not overwhelming, but rather given in small, doable doses.

W hen you insist, they will resist.

J. Knight

Lilian Katz

Maintain an Optimum Distance. Closeness, warmth, and supportiveness are essential and valuable attributes in relationships with teachers. But excessive closeness may inhibit your ability to evaluate a teacher's progress realistically or to confront serious weaknesses. On the other hand, too much distance may make you appear cold or aloof, and this is also unlikely to support a relationship in which growth can occur.

Cultivate the Habit of Suspending Judgment. There is a strong tendency when we observe teachers in the classroom to pass judgment on what we see. We tend not only to judge the rightness or goodness of what we see, but also to assess whether the teacher is doing things "our way." Instead of passing judgment, it may be more helpful to ask oneself, How can I account for what I am observing? Why is the teacher responding to the situation in this way? What are some possible reasons this is happening?

Phrase Your Suggestions in Experimental Form. When observing novice teachers it is sometimes appropriate to offer a helpful suggestion. When giving a suggestion, however, it is best to phrase it not as a directive, but as an option to consider: "Next time X comes up, try Y, and see if it helps." Depending on the situation, you might also want to add, "X helps some teachers in this kind of situation—but if you find it doesn't seem to help, we can talk about something else to try." When a suggestion is offered with the implication that it is the one best solution, and the teacher's attempts to use it subsequently fail, the teacher's sense of frustration and defeat may be intensified rather than diminished.

Avoid the Temptation to Stop Patterns of Behavior. From time to time we observe teacher behavior that we think should be "stopped cold." A two-step approach in such situations may be helpful. First, ask yourself if the behavior observed really endangers any child. If the answer is a clear yes, then the second step is to use all the resources at your disposal to bring the behavior to a halt. If the answer is no, then the next step is to help the teacher try out and practice alternative strategies to replace or supplement the old patterns. If we succeed in stopping a teacher's behavior in advance of sufficient mastery of a new pattern, the teacher may be left without alternative methods of coping with the situation.

Help Teachers Define Their Job So It Is Achievable. Some teachers define their jobs thinking they have to achieve every possible educational objective, or achieve objectives that are almost humanly impossible. For example, many teachers think their job requires them to "love all the children" in their classrooms. But teachers do not have to love or even like all the children they teach—though they do have to respect them all. The latter is not always easy, but is far more achievable than universal love!

Use Demonstrations of Your Own Skills Cautiously. Modeling good practices can be a useful strategy, but modeling is not without some risks. The demonstration of skill may cause some teachers to say to themselves, "I'll never be that good" or "Why is it so easy for her [or him]?," and to become even more discouraged and insecure. These potentially negative consequences must be carefully weighed against the positive value of modeling good practices.

Share Your Understanding of How a Teacher Sees You. We do not always know how the teachers we work with perceive us. Some may see us as warm, sincere, helpful, generous, and giving, but may be unnerved by our presence during observations. If we sense that these feelings are prompted by our presence, it is helpful to let the teacher know that we understand these feelings, that we have also experienced similar feelings, and that we realize teachers might look at us with apprehension, or even fear. Acknowledging the potential for such perceptions can reduce the stress that teachers sometimes experience when being observed.

Adapted from Katz, L. (1993). *Helping others with their teaching*. Urbana, IL: ERIC Clearinghouse on Elementary and Early Childhood Education.

Here are some additional things to cover with new teachers in Phase 2 of the induction process:

- Review hand-washing procedures, norms for greeting children and families, classroom setup, lunch and nap time routines, and use of communication logs.

- Review the center's approach to child guidance, child assessment, and parent relationships.

- Review professional ethics, risk management procedures, and mandated reporting requirements.

- Review the center's annual calendar to understand the yearly schedule, holidays, how curriculum varies over the year, and seasonal special events planned by the center.

- Practice emergency procedures and drills.

- Review scrapbooks, photo albums, or other evidence of the center's history.

Again, this list is not all-inclusive but can serve as a starting place for identifying content and supervisory support strategies to share with new teachers in this phase of the induction process.

Certainly an important goal for this phase of the induction process is to encourage the first-year teacher to become self-reflective through strategically considered questions. It is through self-reflection that new teachers begin to see themselves as competent professionals capable of making appropriate choices relating to curriculum and instruction.

Establish your own professional protocol so that you can maintain mutual respect in your supervisory relationship. That means aligning goals and establishing boundaries for each conversation. Many times conversations take a sour turn because one of the individuals involved is caught off guard about what is going to be covered. No one wants to be blindsided and everyone deserves to intellectually and emotionally prepare for a one-on-one exchange: "At our meeting tomorrow, I'd like to share my observations about Jamie's disruptive behavior during circle time yesterday and get your thoughts about how situations like this might be avoided in the future."

A word about conducting classroom observations: all new teachers are incredibly nervous about having their supervisor or mentor observe them in action. How you approach this process will make the difference in whether your beginning teacher is an eager learner welcoming your fresh perspective or an intimidated subject reluctant to seek help and refine practice. Our recommendation is to focus your observations and to follow-up conversations primarily on what the children are learning and experiencing, rather than what the teacher is doing or not doing. Zeroing in on how the learning environment and how the classroom space is used is another way to take the spotlight off the teacher's behavior and style during this phase of induction.

Conduct informal observations at first, even soliciting teachers' suggestions for what they would like you to focus on. The following Observation Request provides an example. You can focus observations on a single child, social interactions among children, classroom transitions, or interactions between the teacher and a child. The key is to try to observe daily for even a brief 10 to 15 minutes so you get the feel of the rhythm of the classroom.

If your observations are frequent, it won't take long before the teacher develops a comfort level with your presence in the classroom. Until the teacher's confidence is solid, hold off on using any formal classroom observation tools like the Early Childhood Environment Rating Scale–Revised (ECERS-R), the Classroom Learning Assessment Scoring System (CLASS), or the Early Language and Literacy Classroom Observation (ELLCO). These tools will be more appropriate in Phase 3 of the induction process.

Videotaping is another valuable tool for refining practice, but here again let the teacher take the lead. Arrange for videotaping, but initially let the teacher view the videos independently and then share her observations and reflections when she is ready. In their *Exchange* article about powerful interactions, Amy Dombro and her colleagues state that video clips and photos are a mirror you can use to help teachers see moments in their own teaching when they are successful. By "successful" they mean times when teachers connect easily with children, use more language, and elicit more learning from children. A straightforward "I notice ..." statement can call attention to these moments. When you describe what you see, you help teachers become more aware of what they are doing and why it works so they can use it with greater intention.

To help bolster confidence, be sure to honor the new teacher's perspective regarding different organizational practices. There are so many processes we take for granted because we've been doing them a certain way for years. When new teachers are encouraged to question, they can offer a fresh perspective on viewing the center's everyday routines. If their naïve questions are met with a "Wow, we never considered that before," they will feel empowered to contribute more and engage at a deeper level. Treat their simple questions as a gift—an invitation for your experienced teachers to reconsider assumptions and organizational norms in a new light. Dombro and her colleagues underscore the importance of these conversations when they say, "Every interaction you have with a teacher is an opportunity to show the teacher she is heard, respected, and appreciated."

Phase 3: Skill Building

Teachers have many job functions, from planning curriculum, working with parents, organizing the environment, creating teaching materials, to maintaining health and safety guidelines, assessing children's development, and so on. The third phase of induction identifies which job areas should be targeted for focused attention during the second half of the year to help the beginning teacher function more optimally. This is where using formal classroom observation assessments such as the ECERS-R, CLASS, or ELLCO might provide useful data to highlight teachers' areas of strength as well as identify areas to bolster greater intentionality in classroom practices.

At this stage in the induction process teachers should be ready to move into a collaborative relationship in which they are active partners in identifying areas to strengthen as well as different modes for learning that accommodate their learning style and work schedule. This is also the stage when the circle of support can be expanded to include co-workers who can serve as mentors in specific areas that draw out new teachers' strengths.

The approach needs to be individualized because each first year teacher's journey in competence building will be different. For some, viewing DVDs, completing self-paced modules, and reading books or Internet-based resources on specific topics will be appropriate. For others, scheduling time for focused observation of a teacher in another classroom might be in order. Make time to ask your new teachers what methods of learning they liked and why. In general, it is best to keep these skill-building activities close to home. Time spent attending workshops or professional conferences off site can wait until after the first year.

This is also an important time to help the teacher learn how to collect, understand, and use formative assessment and evaluation data to make decisions about individual children and about classroom practices in general. Because early learning standards reflect visions of good teaching, they should also be used to structure conversations about children's learning. As Sharon Feiman-Nemser notes, "When we help new teachers assess their progress toward standards, we induct them into professional habits of inquiry and norms of accountability."

The challenge from a supervisory standpoint is to keep the skill-building goals achievable so the teacher continues to experience incremental success. This is not the time to neglect the one-on-one weekly meetings that will continue to support reflective practice. Use a dedicated hour each week to help teachers deepen their understanding of individual children in their group and strategic ways to use assessment data to scaffold children's learning to the next level of development. Your weekly meetings also provide a structured way for you to offer feedback about how the teacher is doing. Providing timely and meaningful feedback should be a core component of your first year teacher induction program.

Here are a few things to keep in mind when sharing feedback that the teacher may perceive as critical:

- State your feedback respectfully, linking it to the teacher's capacity to grow.
- Focus on behavior, not the person's attitude. Let the teacher know how the behavior impacts the children, other staff, or the center's reputation.
- Be as descriptive and specific as possible, basing your comments on what you have observed, not hearsay from others.
- Focus on the future and describe what you want, not what you don't want.
- Frame your feedback in manageable doses.
- Don't belabor your point.
- Be gentle and discreet.
- Work together to seek solutions or construct options for how the feedback might be used.

Even when the content of your message may be more uplifting, the same tip about being as descriptive and specific as possible applies. In other words, try to avoid a hollow "Good job!" or "Great art project." How much more helpful it is to share with teachers exactly what they did that was of value: "The way you shifted your body and adjusted the book you were reading during circle time allowed the children to see the pictures easily without climbing over one another." It goes without saying, that the interactions you model in providing constructive feedback are those you hope the teachers will demonstrate with the children.

The bumps in the road do not define us. Our mistakes and failures give us the opportunity to discover who we are and who we can become.

Holly Elissa Bruno

Claire and Jenna

Claire is a first-year preschool teacher at Shining Stars Early Learning Center. Jenna, the center's assistant director who oversees the new-teacher induction program, is Claire's supervisor. Jenna feels good about the rapport she has established with Claire. She believes that over the past seven months she has successfully weaned Claire from being heavily dependent on her for advice to where Claire now takes the lead in their weekly conferences to openly reflect on her successes and challenges in working with the children in her classroom.

Jenna felt Claire was ready to have an independent observer come into her classroom to conduct an assessment of instructional practices using the CLASS Pre-K. But when Claire looked over the observer's assessment, she was disheartened at the low rating she received in the dimension Quality of Feedback. Holding back tears, she explained that promoting children's healthy self-esteem was something she really valued. The low score upset her because she thought she was doing a good job praising her students. Rather than dwell on the rating or provide a detailed explanation of the dimension, Jenna asked Claire if she felt it might be useful to analyze some video clips of her teaching during a typical morning of activities.

They made a plan for Jenna to spend a two-hour block of time later that week videotaping a range of one-on-one, small-group, and whole-group activities. When finished, Jenna gave the videotape to Claire and suggested when she viewed it to focus not just on what she was saying or not saying to the children, but also on the children's reactions.

The following week, when the two met, Claire exclaimed, "I was more than a bit nervous to watch myself. I have never been videotaped teaching before." Then she went on to share her insights: "I can't believe how often I say, 'Good job!,' 'Super,' and 'Awesome!' I'm like a bee buzzing around the classroom pollinating the children with praise. At first I thought it was really good, but when I looked at the children's reactions—or better put, lack of reactions—it's like it was going in one ear and out the other."

Jenna was pleased to hear Claire's reflection and posed an open-ended question. "What else might you do when children share their work with you?" Claire struggled a bit with this question and said, "I don't know, I always thought it was important to make children feel good about their work." Jenna then explained that there were some excellent articles in the center's resource library that challenge the notion of too much praise. They discussed Alfie Kohn's alternatives—say nothing, say what you saw, ask more. Claire said she liked the idea of asking more questions and hoped this would help her engage the children in describing and evaluating their own work.

As you wrap up your yearlong new-teacher induction program, be sure to schedule time for the novice teacher to provide you with feedback about your supervisory relationship. Pose questions like, "What strategies have I used this year that helped you become a better teacher?," "What strategies have I used that were not particularly helpful to you?," and "What other ways can I help you?" Such questions not only deepen your understanding about how you can better support this teacher in the future, they also demonstrate your willingness to receive feedback and strengthen your own professional practice.

Novice teacher induction programs are a win-win proposition. Beginning teachers get the support and guidance they need, and experienced staff get the recognition they deserve. In the process, both the novice teacher and the supervisor are compelled to reflect on their own practices and examine their actions and beliefs about teaching and learning. Novice teacher induction programs are a great way to inspire peak performance and strengthen commitment, competence, and collaboration at your center.

Reprinted with permission.

CHAPTER 5

Individual Learning Plans: The Roadmap for Job-Embedded Learning

Imagine a setting where teachers take an active role in determining their learning goals and work in partnership with their supervisor to chart a path for achievement. The goals are rich, meaningful, and relevant to their work, and they serve as roadmaps for building competence and mastery in the classroom. Documenting progress toward achieving their learning goals becomes part of teachers' professional portfolios and is reviewed during their annual performance appraisals.

Most directors understand the value of ongoing professional development. Their own experience confirms what empirical research so indisputably demonstrates— that there is a strong correlation between program stability (as measured by low turnover and high job satisfaction) and a center's commitment to professional development. But even in centers that regularly engage in staff development activities, there seldom exists a coherent philosophy of professional development. In other words, when asked to explain why certain teachers are receiving training on a specific topic or why they attended a particular workshop at a conference, few directors can articulate a rationale for their approach.

A comprehensive model of professional development stands in sharp contrast to the ubiquitous one-size-fits-all on-site training that is characteristic in early childhood programs. What we often see are canned workshops, selected from a smorgasbord of available topics from a local consultant, presented to the entire staff in order to satisfy state licensing requirements. While directors' intentions for hosting these in-service events may be praiseworthy, in most cases, the training itself provides short-lived inspiration for teachers to sharpen their skill set or deepen their understanding of how they can better serve the children in their care and their families.

In many programs, directors create an artificial distinction between work responsibilities and professional development activities. They set aside a few staff development days each year for learning. In contrast, a comprehensive model of professional development supports job-embedded learning where teachers are encouraged to reflect on and address the real-life day-to-day issues they deal with. In this broader view, the work place becomes a laboratory for skill building. *Every* day, not just designated staff development days, holds the potential for rich learning.

Andy Hargreaves captured this sentiment when he said, "What we want for our children we should want for their teachers: that schools be places of learning for both of them, and that such learning be suffused with excitement, engagement, passion, challenge, creativity, and joy." So ask yourself:

- Is your center's approach to staff development tied to a larger vision of what you hope your program will become?

- Do your discussions about professional development focus on the activities you do or the results you achieve?

- Do the professional development experiences at your center challenge you and your staff to think and act in new ways?

A comprehensive model of professional development recognizes that teaching is a complex process in which expertise is gained over an extended period of time. It is not something that is done to teachers, intended to "fix" them or remedy a deficit, but rather something done with teachers to enhance their professional practice and strengthen their commitment to the field.

This chapter zeros in on a key component of a comprehensive model of professional development—individual learning plans. An individual learning plan addresses the issues and concerns that are most important to each teacher, supports the overall mission and vision of the center, builds on previous cycles of learning, and scaffolds teachers to higher levels of professional competence and self-confidence. It is not a document hastily prepared and then tucked away in a file cabinet, but rather a living document that serves as a framework for action.

In this chapter you'll discover why taking the time to develop individual learning plans with each of your teachers can yield rich dividends. You'll learn a step-by-step approach for partnering with teachers to set achievable goals, and suggestions for helping teachers chart their progress in achieving their goals. Before we launch into the details of how to implement individual learning plans in your center, let's recap what we know about why people resist or embrace change.

Change—From Resistance to Compliance to Commitment

We all have tales to tell of resisting change. From the time we were toddlers and asserted emphatically a preference for yellow socks instead of green, we've stood our ground when others have pointed the way to set us straight and try to change us "for our own good." Even when we know a particular change might be good for us, like losing weight or quitting smoking, we often resist. No doubt about it, change is hard.

Change is also fraught with uncertainty. As Tynette Hills quipped, "Each time we ask a person to change, we ask her or him to take a journey into incompetence." So it is not surprising that one of the most common reasons why people resist change is the fear of failure. Whenever we suggest to someone how they might do something differently, we convey the not-so-subtle message that the way they've been doing it is wrong, or at least not good enough. A defensive posture is only natural.

So how do we get people to buy in to change? As a leader it is important for you to remember that there is a big difference between *compliance* and *commitment* when it comes to change. Given the authority of your position, people may change because they believe they have to or because they may want to please you. They may change because the rewards you've set up make it enticing for them to do so. But if you're looking to establish a vibrant professional learning community, you don't want to settle for mere compliance. You want a deeper level of change—commitment. You want people to change because they embrace it as a path to becoming more effective in what they do as teachers. Individual learning plans that honor teachers' voices in identifying areas to strengthen is one promising way to encourage buy in and to achieve a deeper commitment to professional growth.

> People do not resist change. They resist being changed.
>
> *Peter Senge*

The Potential of Individual Learning Plans

Chances are you've experienced firsthand the phenomenon of sending some of your teachers to a local conference or workshop with high hopes it would offer them new insights to help them improve classroom practice. The teachers returned feeling inspired and enthusiastic about the experience, but the next time you observed their classrooms, it was business as usual.

Certainly there is value in allowing teachers to network and learn from others outside your program—to recognize they are members of a dynamic profession. But research backs up what your intuition is telling you—workshops off site, even those of high interest to teachers, have limited impact on changing behaviors unless the professional development experiences include focused follow-up. Individual learning plans help make this happen.

So, what are individual learning plans, and why do they hold so much promise and potential as professional development tools in early childhood programs? In a nutshell, an individual learning plan is a map to navigate a teacher's journey to a deeper level of knowledge and skill in a defined area of learning. Let's take a look at some of the key features of effective learning plans.

Learning plans should be individualized. As the term implies, individual learning plans should be tailored to each teacher's unique background and set of circumstances. When done right, they include differentiated goals and learning opportunities geared to each teacher's career stage, demonstrated level of competence and commitment, preferred learning style, expressed needs, and personal interests.

Learning plans should take a holistic perspective. Plans should treat an individual as a whole person, seeking to strengthen not only the teacher's specific job-related knowledge, skills, and attitudes but also the communication, interpersonal, and life skills needed to support a satisfying and productive career. Expanding understanding of self, role, and context is central to effective professional development.

Learning plans should scaffold teachers' learning. When done right, individual learning plans provide an *optimal mismatch* between what teachers know and can do and what they hope to achieve. By building on strengths, natural talents, and interests, as well as targeted areas for improvement, individual learning plans capitalize on teachers' internal motivations for improving. By honoring teachers' voices, encouraging them to clarify what they need, and partnering with them to create mutually agreed-upon goals, supervisors can empower teachers to take more initiative and responsibility for their own learning and professional development.

Learning plans should be based on meaningful data. Using concrete data to craft learning goals provides a solid rationale for why a teacher is pursuing a particular goal. Data can be from the teacher's self-assessment of perceived gaps in knowledge, self-reports of teaching trouble spots, feedback from parents, informal observations from supervisor and colleagues, or formal observations using research-based assessment tools. Data from children's assessments also provide useful information about areas of instructional support or classroom practices that could be enhanced.

Learning plans should include goals that are achievable and measurable. The tendency for teachers in developing individual learning plans is to envision broad, ambitious goals. But seasoned supervisors know that change is best achieved in small, incremental steps. Defining action steps that are doable within a given time frame is crucial for sustaining teachers' interest and keeping them on track. In other

---

H onoring adults as self-directed learners encourages them to tackle more rigorous improvement goals.

Tony Frontier

words, supervisors should help teachers think big but start small. Most new teachers also need help in framing learning objectives and action steps in ways that allow them to be measured. This is why it is initially good to focus on results that are concrete and tangible to teachers.

Learning plans should build on previous cycles of learning. Each new set of goals, learning objectives, and action steps should be viewed as part of an ongoing professional development spiral of competency building. The plan developed for one year builds on the outcomes from the previous year. These efforts in turn lay the foundation for a plan for the following year. Successive cycles of competency building reinforce the center's norm of continuous quality improvement and the message that learning is a lifelong process.

Learning plans should align with the larger mission and vision of the center. All teachers want to know that their hard work and efforts are not only appreciated but add value to the organization—that teachers are contributing to something larger than themselves. A skillful supervisor helps teachers see how their individual learning goals support centerwide goals and help advance the organization's mission and vision.

Learning plans should align with professional standards. Professional standards provide a framework for understanding best practice and for individual and organizational accountability. In the early childhood arena, this includes state early learning standards for what children should know and be able to do; practitioner standards for teachers' knowledge, skills, and dispositions; and program standards describing the practices of effective early childhood organizations. When supervisors help teachers learn the relevant state and national standards and integrate these into their learning plans, teachers can see how their individual learning goals connect to best practices in the early childhood profession.

Steps in the Process

You already know that haphazard approaches to staff development don't work; neither does simply urging people to do their best. Like other areas of organizational functioning, implementing individual learning plans needs to be approached in a consistent and systematic manner. Just who should guide the process for each teacher depends on the organization's context. In small programs, it is probably you; in larger programs, it may be your assistant director, a teacher's immediate supervisor, or your center's education coordinator.

Determining the schedule for implementing the various steps in the process depends on your program's annual calendar. In programs that follow a 10-month, public school calendar, the process can be set in motion in early September. In year-around programs, you have greater flexibility to structure the cycle according to other supervisory activities in the program.

The three-step process begins with teachers' self-reflection about their current job, their career goals, and the knowledge and skills that might strengthen their overall effectiveness as a teacher. The next step is a planning conference with the teacher to talk about strengths, identify areas for growth, and decide on one or two professional development goals to pursue. The final step involves plotting the action steps and resources needed to achieve the goals and determining criteria for evaluating successful completion.

Appendix B is an Individual Learning Plan template you can use to implement the process at your center. It includes three sections corresponding to the three steps in the process. In the sections that follow, we've included a sample of a completed form for Amber, a preschool teacher who has been working in the field for three years.

Teacher's self-reflection. The first step in the process happens before the teacher and supervisor meet. The purpose of this step is twofold: first, to reinforce the message that staying current in the field and improving effectiveness is part of every teacher's professional obligation; and second, to indicate that the teacher is in the driver's seat in identifying the areas that will become the focus of the learning plan.

Teachers should be encouraged to think about the areas of their job that give them the greatest source of satisfaction and those that are most frustrating. Ask them to try to isolate the aspects of their work that are most problematic and where additional training might help them feel more confident and capable. Encourage them to think about how their current job fits into their overall career plans and how you, their supervisor, can help them take small steps toward achieving their larger career goals.

The teachers will differ in the depth of their reflections. Some teachers may offer fairly superficial responses to the questions compared to others. That is okay. This reflection is not intended to be an academic assignment, merely an opportunity for teachers to think about where they are in their own professional continuum of competence building. The completed reflection sets the stage for the planning conference.

Amber's Individual Learning Plan

Teacher's name: Amber   Date: September 24

Self-Reflection

What aspect of your job gives you the greatest personal satisfaction?

My relationship with the children is my greatest joy. I am lucky to have such a diverse group this year from very different cultural traditions. I also love working with my assistant teacher, Carmen. She has a special way of connecting with the parents of our dual language learners.

What aspect of your job is most frustrating?

With the staffing changes earlier this month, Carmen and I inherited Lila's old classroom. The layout is horrible. The kids are tripping over one another in some areas of the room and other areas are definitely underutilized.

What keeps you from being as effective as you would like to be in your position?

The poor arrangement of space has definitely contributed to some behavioral problems with the children. They are dumping bins of plastic toys all over the place and not really using them in meaningful ways. Cleanup time is a real struggle.

If you had the power to change anything about your job, what would you change?

I think teachers should have more time to get their classrooms set up before new students arrive in September. That didn't happen this year. It would be good if staffing and classroom assignments could be decided earlier next year.

What do you see yourself doing five years from now?

I hope one day to be the lead teacher in the pre-K wing.

What new skills or knowledge would you like to learn this year?

I want to learn how the arrangement of space and small changes in lighting, color, texture, and other design elements impact children's behavior. I'd definitely like to see how I can reduce the amount of plastic in my classroom and introduce more natural elements to make it more calming and aesthetically pleasing.

How can I or other staff help you achieve your personal and professional goals?

I'd like to explore some of the ideas with you that are in two books in our staff library: *Inspiring Spaces for Young Children* and *Designs for Living and Learning*. I'd also like to be able to visit the Reggio-inspired classroom at the community college lab school with you.

Reviewing data and developing goals and objectives. Your initial planning meeting with the teacher sets the tone for the entire process of developing and implementing an individual learning plan. This is the time to hear from the teacher about what is going well and what areas of classroom functioning may be challenging. The underlying assumption of this step is that teachers' personal judgment is a good source of direction for charting individual learning goals. From a developmental supervision perspective, though, teachers may still be in an unconscious incompetence stage of awareness in some areas of professional practice—that is they simply don't know what they don't know and need your guidance and support in identifying potential areas of new learning.

The key is to strike a good balance—focus on areas of strength to build on and identify areas that will expand the teacher's knowledge base and repertoire of skills. This is where the anecdotal notes you have collected from your interactions with the teacher and your informal observations in the classroom become useful. The children's assessment data the teacher has been collecting can provide good clues as to areas of the curriculum that could be strengthened. Data from classroom observations can also provide important information about instructional strategies that could be strengthened or aspects of the physical environment that could be better organized to support children's learning.

When done right, individual learning plans help teachers get a clear understanding of their own strengths and dispositions as well as their professional development needs. The hope is that as you allow teachers more choice and control in structuring their own professional development, they will become more committed to self-improvement and to the center's mission.

Elizabeth Jones uses the phrase *growing teachers* to capture the notion that teacher development is an emergent, open-ended process where philosophy and practice are defined, but outcomes are less clear. Similarly, implementing individual learning plans rests on the premise that teachers are active agents in constructing knowledge about their work and need to be involved in making choices about options for their personal and professional growth. This means that each plan should embody the expressed hopes and aspirations of the teacher.

By the end of this initial planning meeting the teacher should have identified a growth area to focus on and a learning goal to achieve during the next six to nine months. If the goal is going to be meaningful, it must be moderately challenging and not something that could be achieved after just a few weeks of effort. Likewise, it shouldn't be so bold and audacious that the teacher will feel overwhelmed and unable to achieve it during the designated time frame.

The goal is to develop everyone's 'yearning for learning' for a lifetime.

J. Bosting

When directors include teachers in goal setting, they express confidence in them, communicating the powerful message that they believe they are reliable sources of information. It makes sense. When teachers are able to define their own problems to solve or identify a special learning goal to pursue, their commitment to following through will be greater than if someone else directs their learning. Goals need not be grandiose, but they do need to be meaningful. Your teachers' time is valuable, so goals can't be frivolous; they must have value for the individual.

Help your teachers think of their goal statement as the destination of where they want to get to—their vision of what the improved situation will look like. Once they have articulated their goal, help them specify two or three objectives for each goal that they hope to achieve. Objectives are statements that define measureable, observable behaviors that lead toward a goal and are typically stated in phrases that begin with the word *to*. While goals are broad statements of what the teacher hopes to accomplish, objectives are more precise statements of what needs to be done to achieve a specific goal.

The goals teachers define should clearly fit where they are in the developmental continuum of professional competence. Teachers in the early stages of their careers will zero in on goals that are practical and specifically targeted to help them cope with the challenges they face daily in the classroom. Master teachers, however, will think more expansively and should be encouraged to stretch themselves beyond the borders of their classroom, thinking of learning goals that will bolster their skill in mentoring others, facilitating meetings, presenting, or taking on a leadership role in professional associations.

The final activity in this initial goal-setting session is to define the professional standard or standards that the goal relates to. This could be from NAEYC's accreditation standards and criteria or professional preparation standards, the Head Start Child Development and Early Learning Framework, or your state's early learning standards. This step is important because it ties the teacher's learning plan to the early childhood profession's standards for best practice, thus reinforcing how this single learning plan contributes to the professionalization of the early childhood workforce.

Putting teachers' learning goals and objectives in writing is important because it helps formalize the process and strengthen their commitment to the next step— writing an action plan to make the objectives come alive.

Becoming an expert teacher is not a gift bestowed on a chosen few, but a journey through a challenging, thorny pathway that requires constant pruning.

Paul Mielke

Goal Setting

Strengths as a teacher

1. Creates a nurturing emotional climate for children
2. Supports assistant teacher through effective modeling and helpful feedback
3. Promotes a spirit of teamwork in the pre-K wing

Identified growth areas

1. I'd like to expand my understanding about how the classroom space is currently being used and how it could be reconfigured to be more engaging and conducive to learning.
2. I want to learn how different design elements like color, texture, light, and objects from nature can be integrated into the learning environment to make it more aesthetically pleasing.
3. I'd like to explore how to weave examples from the children's cultural heritages into the classroom environment.

Goal

The classroom space will be a warm and engaging learning environment that reflects the cultural diversity of the children served.

Related standards

NAEYC Early Childhood Program Accreditation Standards and Criteria

3.A. Designing enriched learning environments

7.A. Knowing and understanding the program's families

2.J. Curriculum content area for cognitive development: Creative expression and appreciation for the arts

Objectives

1. To improve the use of space during free-choice time
2. To increase the use of natural elements in the classroom environment and decrease reliance on plastic and commercially produced materials
3. To increase the ways that children's cultural heritages are reflected in the environment

Writing action steps. The final step in helping teachers develop their individual learning plans is to detail the activities that will be carried out in order to achieve each objective. This involves several decisions, such as estimating the time that should be allocated for each activity, the resources needed, and how the anticipated outcomes will be evaluated. Think of the action steps as different strategies teachers can use that together will accomplish the objective. There are so many possibilities. Teachers can

- read professional books and journal articles
- participate in online webinars and blogs
- attend off-site workshops or in-depth institutes
- view DVDs and online videos
- take a college course
- conduct classroom research
- observe other teachers at the center
- observe classrooms at other centers
- work with a coach on a focused area of the curriculum
- maintain a reflective journal
- participate in a peer learning team
- observe and reflect on video clips of themselves in action

Your role in helping teachers determine the appropriate strategies and resources needed to achieve their learning goals depends on many factors. After all, each teacher is a unique individual with different experiences, skills, and interests. Teachers naturally gravitate to those activities that best support their individual learning style, so use this opportunity to help them also consider options that will stretch them beyond their comfort zone.

The center's financial resources also impact the range of options that can be considered. In some centers each teacher is allocated a professional development stipend that can be used to cover expenses related to their individual learning plan. You can also help teachers tap into available professional development resources from your local resource and referral agency that can be used to cover costs associated with college tuition and registration fees for conferences, and for expenses related to pursuing their professional development goals. Release time to observe other classrooms, visit other programs, or attend conferences have a dollar value that needs to be considered if substitutes are hired to cover a teacher's absence.

Amber's Individual Learning Plan (continued)

Action Steps

Objective #1: To improve the use of space during free-choice time

Activities	Time needed	Resources needed
• Do an observation of how the children currently use different learning centers during free-choice time • Based on the findings, rearrange the classroom to achieve better overall balance in the use of learning centers • Document changes in a second observation in 3 months	• 4 hrs to gather initial data • 2 hours to draw up new plan and 8 hrs over a weekend to rearrange classroom • 4 hrs to gather data documenting change	• 4 hrs of floater time to help out during data collection • Someone to help rearrange space • 4 hours of floater time for post analysis

Evaluation: Share initial findings and plan for redesign with my supervisor in October. Discuss findings from post analysis and share journal reflections of the change process in May.

Objective #2: To increase the use of natural elements in the classroom environment and decrease reliance on plastic and commercially produced learning materials

Activities	Time needed	Resources needed
• Conduct a self-study of classroom using the Rating Observation Scale for Inspiring Environments (ROSIE), visit Reggio-inspired classroom at the college lab school, and read four articles • Participate in "Going Green" webinar • Make 2 changes each week to reduce plastic and add more natural elements	• 2 hrs to do self-study and 4 hours for site visit • 4 hours to read books and articles • 2 hrs per week to gather materials and make changes	• Copy of ROSIE • 4 hrs of substitute time • $80 to purchase baskets, fabric, pillows, and miscellaneous items from thrift store

Evaluation: Share results of self-study with my supervisor in October. Take photographs weekly to document changes.

Objective #3: To increase the ways children's cultural heritage is reflected in the environment

Activities	Time needed	Resources needed
• Invite families to share photographs, books, fabric, musical instruments, and other artifacts reflecting their cultural heritage • Display cultural items as appropriate and weave into curriculum	• 20 min per family • 15 min/wk to update displays with new items	• 20 min of Carmen's time per week to connect with Spanish-speaking families

Evaluation: Share progress with supervisor and peer learning team in February

Usually the hardest part for teachers is to determine how they want to measure the accomplishment of each objective detailed in their plan. If the outcome is tangible, evidence of the product or final project will be sufficient; but if the goal is a change in behavior, then some thought and consideration will need to be put into how to best evaluate the change desired.

Individual learning plans often need refining as they are being implemented. People get sick, workshops are cancelled, and circumstances change. For this reason it's important that you and your teachers stay flexible, making changes as needed. Depending on how large your program is, you may be the key person monitoring the individual learning plans that have been initiated. Without exercising leadership on your part, the entire process may crumble. Staff development does not happen just by talking about it. There must be active follow-through to keep the process moving and relevant.

In this chapter we've seen how individual learning plans can help transform teachers' beliefs, attitudes, and instructional practices and the center's culture. Margie Carter reminds us that the work of feeding the hearts and minds of young children is multifaceted, requiring constant negotiation of the intricate intersection between theory and practice. Likewise, we believe that feeding the hearts and minds of teachers is a powerful means for elevating their knowledge and skill and reinforcing the disposition of curiosity and lifelong learning.

When implemented in a systematic and thoughtful way, individual learning plans can also have a ripple effect throughout the entire center if teachers have the opportunity to share the outcome of their efforts with others. One way to multiply the impact of professional learning is to weave in structured opportunities during your regularly scheduled staff meetings for teachers to share what they learn. In the next chapter we talk about the potential of peer learning teams as another way to accomplish the goal of paying it forward.

CHAPTER 6

Peer Learning Teams: The Platform for Collegial Support

Imagine a workplace where teachers feel safe, comfortable, and eager to share their insights, struggles, and goals with one another. Where you walk down the hall and see teachers from various classrooms gathered in lively conversation about children's learning. Here is an environment where the joy of learning unfolds at all levels of the organization; where colleagues encourage and support each other's growth through meaningful collaboration.

We live in a global village with the amazing capacity to connect through technology and social media; yet so many people say they feel isolated and alone. Even in many work settings people have little substantive interaction with their colleagues. Judith Warren Little has referred to the landscape of schools as "individual classrooms connected by a common parking lot." While her critique was focused on elementary and secondary schools, the situation in many early childhood programs is no different.

If you are intent on creating a professional learning community and strengthening norms of collaboration at your center, then it seems important to stop the madness, so to speak, and navigate a manageable course to enable your teachers to break down the walls of isolation. One promising approach is to set up peer learning teams.

This chapter provides a road map for how to set up collaborative learning teams to keep the learning spirit alive. It provides practical advice on what peer-to-peer learning is and why it is such a useful model for early childhood programs. Most importantly, the chapter guides you on how to get started offering strategies for success.

What Are Peer Learning Teams and Why Do They Matter?

There are a variety of terms used for this type of small-group work, including *study groups*, *communities of practice*, *learning communities*, and *peer-to-peer technical assistance*. The truth is, all of them are variations on the same theme. They all embody practices that create a context and place for collaboration and professional growth. Optimally these small groups put to use standards, assessments, and data to assist in the learning process through intentional reflection. In this book, we use the term *peer learning teams* to focus on the specific small-group work accomplished within a center-based program.

Learning teams are best defined as ongoing groups of four or five teachers that meet regularly with the focus on increasing understanding about children's learning. Members of a team value theory and best practice and encourage each other to try out new ideas, reflect on what works and why, and construct new knowledge. Joellen Killion tells us the goal of this type of peer-to-peer learning is to create a meaningful professional development experience aligned with constructivist theory. This includes opportunities to co-construct knowledge, share experiences, reflect on practice, seek feedback, and contribute to the learning of others.

As you learned in Chapter 5, many teachers indicate that the professional development they receive makes little difference to them. Perhaps a new model that more actively engages them in their daily work is a better approach. It makes good sense that teachers will thrive and grow in their knowledge when provided a collegial forum to contemplate and grapple with issues related to children's learning. Why is it then that so many teachers within the same center work in isolation with almost complete autonomy?

Sharon Feiman-Nemser says that without structured opportunities and easy access to one another, teachers may feel reluctant to share problems or ask for help, believing that good teachers figure things out on their own. Teachers may not realize the potential of this kind of learning synergy because they haven't experienced the value of sharing ideas and building on the experiences and knowledge of others. Even when teachers do get together, they may not know how to engage in productive talk about teaching and learning. Often concerns for comfort and harmony lead teachers to minimize differences in philosophy or practice and avoid offering an alternative perspective.

Breaking down the isolation and establishing learning teams also provides a positive impact on teacher retention. In a research study of the Chicago Public Schools, Elaine Allensworth and her colleagues found that the quality of the work environment was strongly predictive of whether teachers remained at their schools. One key element in retention was teachers' perceptions of their colleagues as collaborators. Teachers were more likely to stay at a school if they saw themselves as part of a team that was working together toward making their school better, supported by school leadership.

Offering meaningful professional development through collaboration with co-workers and increasing the odds for greater teacher retention are excellent reasons for wanting to establish learning teams in your program. So, what is needed to get started?

Getting Started—Some Things to Think About

No doubt many good ideas and well-meaning intentions have come and gone in your program. After all, part of good leadership is being innovative and willing to try new ideas to spark inspiration and continuous quality improvement. How do you go about determining whether learning teams are a worthwhile model to consider for your staff? There are three steps that will help you know: assess your team's readiness, articulate a rationale, and decide on the appropriate structure that will ensure success.

Assessing team readiness. Not all programs are a good fit for implementing learning teams. Before launching into this approach, first assess your program's level of readiness to engage in peer learning teams. Here are a few critical questions to consider in determining whether this model of professional development is a good fit for you and your staff:

- Do your teachers demonstrate an interest in continued improvement and the joy of refining their craft?

- Does your organizational climate promote a high level of collegiality? Are your teachers friendly, supportive, and trusting of one another?

- Do teachers have a shared understanding of your center's core values?

- Do teachers exhibit a deep and genuine interest in children's learning?

- Are you willing to modify work schedules so teachers have time to meet on a regular basis?

If you can answer yes to these five questions, there is greater likelihood you'll experience success in implementing learning teams in your program.

Articulating a rationale. The second step is to communicate to your teachers a rationale for doing this work and inviting them to participate. It includes articulating a clear and compelling message for the use of peer learning teams in your program. There are many reasons why directors implement learning teams at their centers. Here is an exercise to help consolidate your reasons for pursuing this kind of work.

Exercise 6

Read through the following reasons and select the **two** that best describe why introducing peer learning teams at your center might be a good program strategy for continuous quality improvement.

☐ To create a collaborative culture that focuses on thinking more deeply about children's learning and interests

☐ To provide an ongoing support system for teachers to help them learn and grow

☐ To help teachers build leadership skills like group facilitation, active listening, probing for understanding, and providing feedback in a respectful way

☐ To help teachers make meaning out of early learning standards, assessments, and data

☐ To foster a collective commitment to the center's core value of continuous improvement.

☐ To strengthen centerwide collegiality

☐ To encourage intentional teaching practices that link theory to practice

Now you have a clearer sense of why learning teams might be a viable approach for your center. This will help you build your vision and articulate to your team the purpose of this work.

Deciding on structure. The third step in getting started is to determine group size, composition, and the frequency that the peer learning teams will meet. Being intentional about allocating time is essential. Remember the secret to success in this small-group work is that the groups meet regularly over an extended period of time. Engage your teachers in brainstorming possibilities for when groups could meet, or consider allocating time at your regularly scheduled staff meetings for learning team work. Ideally one hour every two weeks would be devoted for learning team meetings. This may seem like a big commitment at first, but once teachers experience firsthand the power of being part of a learning team, they become invested in finding time to meet.

We have found that the optimum size for learning teams is four or five members. The composition of groups will vary depending on your organizational context and specific organizational improvement goals. Consider forming groups in which members have mixed roles or similar roles, mixed levels of experience or similar levels of experience, or mixed age levels taught or same age levels taught. There is no right or wrong way to configure the composition of groups. We recommend that teams work together for a year. It is the ability to meet together over an extended period of time that forges the best opportunities for meaningful engagement. The following year, consider a different group composition.

Promoting Participation, Ensuring Equity, and Building Trust

By now it should be clear that implementing structured teams to promote collaborative learning is far different from the kind of casual collegial exchanges that take place during lunch or on breaks in your teachers' lounge. As Joseph McDonald and his colleagues state, "The kind of talking needed to educate ourselves cannot arise spontaneously and unaided from just talking. It needs to be carefully planned and scaffolded." They explain, "At its heart, a leader's role in facilitating a learning community is to promote participation, ensure equity, and build trust." Let's consider each of these goals more deeply.

Promoting participation. The aim of promoting participation is to encourage an open forum for considering multiple perspectives to deepen individual and group understanding. It also consolidates knowledge when teachers are given an opportunity to articulate their own perceptions. A key element to promoting participation is establishing a set of ground rules. Rather than imposing a uniform set of guidelines for all groups, we have found it works best if each peer learning team establishes its own set of rules.

One way to get the conversation going about desired group norms is to have team members reflect back on their best and worst experiences in group discussions. What were the things that happened that made some of those experiences so satisfying and others frustrating? What lessons can be drawn from those previous experiences about the group norms team members would like to have for their learning team?

Learning is at once deeply personal and inherently social: it connects us not just to knowledge in the abstract, but to each other.

Peter Senge

Shining Stars Early Learning Center

Ground Rules for Learning Team #1

We will . . .

- Make sure that each person has time to speak
- Be present as fully as possible
- Listen to understand different points of view
- Participate without dominating
- Avoid judgmental comments
- Learn to respond with honest, open questions
- Treat each other as equals
- Be comfortable with silence
- Maintain confidentiality
- Be open to possibility
- Encourage all voices to be heard

Ensuring equity. The very practice of bringing a number of people together means there will be diverse learning styles and temperaments at the table. It is easy in small-group gatherings for one person's voice and point of view to dominate the discussion. Ensuring equity in group interactions stems from the desire to encourage divergent thinking. Learning to listen with positive intentionality and being open to contrary viewpoints helps foster the groups' learning process.

In high-performing groups, norms of collaboration are exhibited by members regardless of role or title. The most productive groups are those where members make a conscious commitment to practice communication strategies that honor every voice and perspective.

Ways to Support Learning Conversations

- Advocate for your ideas, but resist the temptation to state your position repeatedly.

- Make sure your contributions are relevant to the discussion.

- Wait until others have finished talking before jumping into the conversation.

- Ask questions to clarify facts and to better understand people's beliefs and assumptions.

- Pause after asking a question to allow time for people to think before they respond.

- Paraphrase frequently to summarize what has been said and ensure everyone is on the same page.

- Presume that others have positive intentions.

- Disagree respectfully.

Building trust. Working in a peer learning team is a relationship-based experience. A vital component of any type of relationship is a sense of trust. Because your teachers may have worked together at your center for a while, you might assume they have already established trusting relationships. But this may not necessarily be the case. The kind of deep, trusting relationships needed for an effective learning team are different from the congenial relationships typical among staff in early childhood programs.

In their book *The Power of Protocols*, Joseph McDonald and his colleagues say that the goal is not just to have team members trust one other as individuals, but also to trust the situation that has been collectively created. In other words, the goal is not to make everyone feel comfortable, but rather to know that individuals can learn from each other and work together even when the work creates discomfort—as work involving worthwhile learning often does.

One way to build trust is to create a safe space where individuals have an opportunity to reflect and share stories. An activity to get this started with a new learning team is to invite members to generate a list of milestones in their professional journey—five or six significant events that have shaped their careers or challenges that side tracked them along the way. Invite them to write a little about the importance of each milestone and then share these reflections with other team members.

The Facilitator—A Key Player in Supporting Team Success

Peer learning teams are most successful when there is a facilitator, sometimes referred to as a *critical friend,* assigned to guide the group in its work. Initially, you will want to invite one member of the team to take on this role. After the group gets going, members can rotate the responsibility. That way each person will have an opportunity to develop the important leadership skill of facilitating.

The facilitator needs to have a clear understanding that this work is different from coaching or mentoring. The aim is not to be the expert but to promote participation, ensure equity, and build trust. Thus, all team members, regardless of experience, education, or titles, have the potential to be skilled facilitators.

The role of the facilitator is to support the group's thinking and learning. This means listening and posing questions and comments to guide the group, broadening the conversation, and summarizing key points. The goal is to create a sense of community that values all ideas and comments. The facilitator ensures that all voices in the group are heard, and that the group considers different ideas and perspectives. The facilitator is also timekeeper and has the task of keeping the group focused and moving along.

The Learning Team at Work

These days it seems early childhood education is moving on two parallel tracks: a push toward early learning standards, assessments, and data linked to child outcomes on one track, and a desire to support more intentional, reflective teaching practices on the other track. How then do you promote a professional learning community where teachers can learn and grow on these parallel tracks of standards, assessments, and data while still being intentional and reflective in their work? The answer is peer learning teams. Peer learning teams hold the potential for merging these two tracks into one.

Here are three general topics that will help get your learning teams rolling. A team could focus on a single topic for the entire year they are together or decide to use a more eclectic approach, exploring different topics during the course of their time together.

Core values in practice. Most teachers are pretty good at articulating their program's educational philosophy and mission. After all, these are usually highlighted in the center's parent and staff handbooks. It is a bit more challenging, though, for teachers to articulate the center's core values that provide the foundation for the program's philosophy and mission. And even more challenging to describe how these core values are put into practice in the classroom. A center may embrace core values like cooperation, excellence, creativity, fairness, and responsibility, but what do these values look like in action?

If one of the goals of professional development is to help teachers articulate a rationale for the different instructional decisions they make hour-by-hour, day-by-day in their classrooms, then exploring the link between the center's core values and different classroom practices can help promote greater intentionality. No doubt about it, programs where teachers are more intentional in the way they prepare the learning environment and interact with children and families are also more successful participating in state quality rating and improvement initiatives or achieving center accreditation.

A learning team agenda that focuses on core values can lead to rich discussions about the role of the teacher, the layout of the classroom, how time is allocated during the day, and which instructional strategies best support children's learning. An exploration of core values can be done over several months by shining the spotlight on one teacher's classroom during each session. The teacher can videotape a short segment of classroom practice or take five or six photographs capturing images of core values in action.

Using the following protocol will help ensure that the discussion is objective, that the teacher is never put on the defensive, and that all members of the team walk away with a deeper understanding about how core values can drive instructional decision making. When the learning team convenes, the teacher presents the video clip or photographs for the other team members to view. This is done without any commentary. The goal is to have the other team members have their first look at the images in silence. Then one-by-one the team members answer the questions below as the teacher listens to their analysis:

- As you viewed the video clip or looked at the photographs, what did you see?

- What questions do the images raise for you?

- What core values might the images represent?

- How does the video clip or the photographs connect with your own ideas about the care and education of young children?

After listening to the team members' perspectives about the video clip or photographs, the teacher reflects on what new themes or ideas were sparked by the discussion. The intent of the teacher's response is not to provide a rationale for the specific video clip or photographs, but rather to share what was learned by listening to how others perceived the images. This experience can strengthen teachers' understanding of their work. Results of this activity are usually eye-opening. Teachers become aware of the direct connection between what the center preaches and what is practiced. They also become more attuned to other perspectives and how actions are perceived. This new-found awareness leads to more intentionality and clarity in what they do.

Assessment tools. Most states have now established quality rating and improvement systems (QRIS) for center-based programs serving young children. Typically, a component of the process is to have an assessment conducted using a valid and reliable tool such as the CLASS or ECERS-R. Clearly, a program has a greater rate of success with QRIS if teachers have a comprehensive knowledge of the assessment tools being used.

Appendix C includes a copy of a form titled "Getting to Know the Assessment Tool" that your teachers can use to guide their discussions about the different items included in a particular instrument. In this section we've included a completed example from one teacher whose learning team delved deeper into understanding specific dimensions included in the CLASS. Dissecting the tool over several months helped members of the learning team understand the rationale behind different dimensions and explore how their own classrooms could be strengthened to meet the established criteria.

Each member of the team completed the form for the dimension scheduled for discussion. When they met and each shared their understanding of the dimension, common themes began to emerge and a deeper understanding of the value and intention of the dimension became clear. Here are the questions that guided their discussion:

- What are common beliefs we agree upon relating to this item or dimension of the tool?

- Are there any areas where we have differing points of view?

- What resources might help guide our group to a better understanding of this dimension?

- Are there steps we'd like to take to improve this dimension in our classrooms?

Teacher: Marta   **Date:** September 23

Assessment tool: CLASS Pre-K

Item or dimension: Instructional Learning Formats

Why does this item matter for positive child outcomes?
While we want children to have fun play experiences, we also want them to be actively learning.

Key questions prompted by the item	The environment includes	A child will experience
• Am I involved, asking meaningful questions and expanding children's interests? • Do the children have a wide range of hands-on materials that peak their curiosity? • When I scan the room, are children actively engaged in activities? • Can the children explain what they are learning?	• Teachers moving around and working with the children • Lots of materials and experiences for kids to explore, like the new recycled art materials I put out on the art shelf this week	• Never being bored or sitting around waiting! • Active, hands-on learning

When you think about this item in your own environment, what questions come up?

I think I do a pretty good job with the dimension Instructional Learning Formats during free choice time. But I'm not so sure how well I do during group time. It feels like I spend a lot of time correcting children's behavior and trying to get them to listen. They often seem tuned out. I wonder what a high score in this CLASS dimension looks like during group time.
I would also like to learn more about the effective facilitation indicator within this dimension. What do they mean by "effective questioning?"

What steps are necessary to implement or improve this item in your environment?

Perhaps I could observe one of Sam's group times? During our learning team sessions he has described some pretty interesting things he's done with the children when they gather as a whole group.

I wonder if our learning team could review some of the CLASS video clips that focus on effective facilitation. The videos might offer some concrete examples. If I'm not sure about this concept, others might be struggling too.

Early learning standards. Our approach to early care and education has evolved over the past few decades as the mantra for greater accountability at the federal and state levels has spawned the development of standards to guide practice. In Head Start and state-funded pre-K programs, teachers no longer simply set up interesting learning environments and trust that children will master the knowledge and skills needed for kindergarten readiness. The emphasis now is on teachers being intentional about what and how children learn by linking their curriculum and instructional strategies to early learning standards. The expectation is not that all children must achieve certain standards at the same time, but rather that these guideposts support teachers in offering meaningful learning environments to meet the needs of each and every child.

Here is a peer learning team activity that links early learning standards to classroom practice with intention and meaning. The first step is to select a video clip of children in a classroom that demonstrates developmentally appropriate practice. (In the references at the end of this book we've included several sources where you can access video clips.) The learning team will also want a copy of the state's early learning standards or the Head Start Child Development and Early Learning Framework as a resource.

In watching the video clip, team members should focus on the children's learning experience rather than critiquing the teacher. The following questions can serve as a guide for the ensuing discussion:

- What resonates with you about the children's learning when viewing this video clip?

- Did you see evidence of any early learning standards in practice in this video clip?

- If you were the teacher in this classroom, how might you document this as evidence of a child achieving a certain benchmark?

- What teaching strategies might this teacher consider to further enrich children's learning and meet additional learning standards?

- Does this video remind you of something you have done in your classroom that links to an early learning standard?

Devoting time to specific topics of interest is a good mechanism for keeping a learning team on task and focused. Above we offered a few such topics including core values, classroom assessment tools, and learning standards. Clearly, there are many more topics that could be explored.

Reflecting on Learning

Throughout this book we have underscored the importance of reflection as a vital component of professional development. It is so easy in the rush of daily obligations to skip this essential step in the learning cycle. Reflecting on practice is what deepens the learning experience and helps individuals make connections to other areas of inquiry that might expand perceptions and alter practice. The mere act of writing down what transpired can also reinforce key concepts learned and strengthen teachers' resolve to make changes.

Encourage your teachers to take time after each learning team session to reflect on both the content of what was covered and the group meeting process. These reflections can be added to the teachers' professional portfolio, documenting professional growth, a topic we'll explore in the next chapter.

"Have you ever noticed all the comfort food
in a teachers lounge?"

Shining Stars Early Learning Center
Learning Team Reflection

Learning Team: Preschool #1   **Date of meeting:** May 20
Team Member: Marta

The purpose of this team meeting:

To reflect on core values.

The data or artifact that focused our thinking was:

Barbara's video clip of her group time about butterflies.

Something that helped to foster trust within our group was:

Sam shared his frustration when children lose interest during a group activity.

An example where we challenged our thinking or took differing points of view within the group:

We were focused on the children's behavior during group time, and Rosa questioned whether a group time at the end of day was necessary. This led to an intense discussion of the value of group time and how many whole-group gatherings are needed in one day.

My participation in this meeting was:

Intense. I caught myself interrupting others and taking over the conversation. Next time I will try to do more listening and be open to other points of view, even though I have the most years of teaching experience on our team.

One idea I'm excited to try in my own classroom based on this conversation:

Converting one of my group times into a small-group activity. This will provide an opportunity for more focused learning.

We were successful in:

Following the cues of our facilitator. Sam did a good job of keeping us focused and starting and ending our meeting on time.

CHAPTER 7

360-Degree Feedback: A Catalyst for Growth and Change

MarcArt

Imagine a performance appraisal system at your center where the full weight of evaluating performance did not fall on your shoulders alone— a process that valued multiple perspectives in evaluating individual and collective performance. Picture an evaluation system that elevates the role of team members in which each person not only receives but also provides helpful feedback to others. The feedback is specific in providing a broader understanding of how each person contributes to and impacts the center's mission.

It's no surprise that in most organizations, performance appraisal is a dreaded activity not just for the employee, but also for the supervisor. Many supervisors confess they feel ill-equipped to handle the daunting responsibility of conferring judgment, particularly when evaluation is tied to contract renewal or compensation decisions. The problem in a nutshell is that in most organizations, performance appraisal is a top-down process that is divorced from professional development. It doesn't need to be this way. When the evaluation of performance is ongoing and viewed as part of the center's larger goal of continuous quality improvement, it can serve as a powerful catalyst for growth and change. Instead of being a dreaded activity, it can be a welcome and celebrated process.

There are two things that distinguish the evaluation process in high-performing early childhood programs that function like true professional learning communities. First, evaluation and professional development activities are integrated and take place continuously during the year. Second, teachers are treated with respect and have an active voice and key role in the evaluation process. With some modifications in the traditional approach to performance appraisal, your center can achieve this broader vision.

This chapter explores how 360-degree feedback can be woven into your center's performance appraisal process, helping to make it more robust and meaningful. We begin the discussion by first reviewing the principles of effective performance appraisal and describing the difference between formative and summative evaluation. Then we look at how multiple sources of evidence in a 360-degree approach can improve the reliability of performance appraisal. Finally, we offer some suggestions about how to nurture a culture of appreciation. As in previous chapters, the examples used in this chapter relate to teachers, but the practices are certainly applicable to your administrative and support staff as well.

Performance Appraisal—A Vital Function in High-Performing Organizations

Every person who works for an organization wants to know the answer to two questions: What do you expect of me? And how am I doing in meeting your expectations? Sadly, in many early childhood programs these two questions are treated so perfunctorily they miss the potential for inspiring peak performance and, in some cases, contribute to role confusion and employee dissatisfaction. The answer to the first question is a generic job description handed out during the hiring process. The answer to the second question comes from the supervisor's evaluation at the end of the year, based on a quick observation of teaching and the completion of a generic performance rating form. No wonder teachers use words like biased, incomplete, arbitrary, and even humiliating to describe their annual performance evaluation experience.

In a professional learning community, the answer to these two questions is quite different. The first question, "What do you expect of me?," is answered at the start of the year when supervisors meet to review each teacher's job description, discuss goals, and develop individual learning plans. This is the time when the nuances in performance criteria are clarified. Teachers not only know what is expected of them, but they also have a clear understanding of the role they will play in gathering relevant data during the year to provide evidence of their performance and professional growth.

The answer to the second question, "How am I doing in meeting your expectations?," is provided at several points throughout the year when supervisors meet with teachers to review their performance, discuss progress in meeting learning goals, and make modifications as needed to accommodate changing conditions in their classroom and the context of their work. The supervisor and teacher meet again at the end of the year for a formal review of performance in which teachers share accomplishments, document their learning and the learning of children in their classroom, and begin the next cycle of charting new areas of professional growth.

This description of an integrated professional development and performance appraisal system embodies both formative and summative evaluation.

- **Formative evaluation** is informal and ongoing—the purpose is to build competence and commitment to continued learning. The focus of formative evaluation is to provide constructive feedback, recognize and reinforce outstanding practice, and unify staff around a collective vision of how to best support children's learning.

- **Summative evaluation** is more formal and occurs usually only once a year, and the purpose is to support accountability. The annual formal review is a legal process designed to provide a summary of the teacher's performance against established criteria and serve as the basis for contractual decisions. The focus of summative evaluation is on quality assurance and providing legally defensible evidence for personnel retention and dismissal decisions.

Programs need both formative and summative evaluation, but clearly through the lens of inspiring peak performance, the emphasis should be on ensuring robust opportunities for formative evaluation—evaluation that supports a teacher's ongoing growth and development. If performance appraisal is viewed as an ongoing activity during the year, then there should be no surprises at the annual summative evaluation.

Let's be clear. There is no one right way to evaluate people. Every early childhood program needs to develop forms and procedures that are appropriate for its unique context. A good evaluation system should not be complicated.

The following principles are adapted from *Blueprint for Action: Achieving Center-Based Change through Staff Development*, and they provide a starting point for thinking about the formative and summative evaluation practices in your center. *Blueprint for Action* provides a more extensive treatment of the subject and even includes examples of how performance appraisal can be tied to a career ladder.

Performance appraisal must be thorough. Because time is such a scarce commodity for early childhood administrators, it is tempting to cut short the time needed for meeting one-on-one with teachers to provide feedback and review progress in meeting targeted goals. But when viewed through the lens of program effectiveness, the time allocated to evaluating staff pays tremendous dividends. Interestingly, this is an area teachers feel strongly about. They are hungry to have their hard work validated and feel short-changed when the evaluation process isn't treated seriously.

Performance appraisal must be fair. One of the quirks of human nature is our tendency to let personal biases cloud our judgment. In evaluating staff performance, personal biases can sabotage your goal of implementing a system that is perceived by all staff as objective.

Both the criteria you use to evaluate performance and the process of conducting a performance appraisal must be perceived as fair. That is why clear rubrics that describe specific results the person has achieved or metrics that focus on the frequency of a behavior (*seldom, sometimes, often, always*) are better than metrics that measure subjective traits and are open to different interpretations (*poor, satisfactory, excellent*).

Effective performance appraisal depends on clear job descriptions. A clear and concise job description provides the foundation for a fair and accurate evaluation. In many programs job descriptions are given out during the hiring or orientation process, never to be seen again. This is unfortunate because job descriptions are an important means of ensuring accountability. When reviewed annually to capture the core functions of a teacher's role, a job description can serve as an effective tool for helping the teacher succeed.

A clear job description can provide baseline data for the level of expected performance because job descriptions, when done right, provide a concise picture of the competencies the employee needs. Thus job descriptions for teachers of infants, toddlers, and school-age children should be slightly different.

Staff should be actively involved in developing evaluation criteria. Because the context of each early childhood program is different, the performance appraisal criteria need to reflect the unique values, culture, and goals of the program. If the evaluation method is to accurately measure the knowledge, skills, and attitudes of the staff, then teachers need to have an integral role in determining how their performance should be evaluated.

Performance appraisal should build on the competencies of the individual. Evaluation must be viewed as a helping process—a time for building awareness and aspiring to new goals—rather than as a punitive process. From a motivation standpoint, focusing on a teacher's deficits is simply counterproductive. Feedback that builds on a teacher's strengths changes the nature of the interaction to one of looking at potential. In the end, this is what moves individuals to higher levels of performance and a stronger sense of self-efficacy and confidence.

Performance appraisal should focus on behavior but not ignore traits and dispositions. In defining behaviors, be mindful that the specific criteria are sufficiently precise to provide a useful benchmark for performance. For example, *communicates with parents* as a criterion for judging performance is too vague to measure. Does this mean saying hello and goodbye as parents drop off their children each day, or does it mean weekly progress notes home, a monthly newsletter, and two parent conferences a year? Without more specific behavioral descriptors added to the criteria, a supervisor and teacher may have conflicting expectations of just what each criterion really means.

Traits such as *friendly, responsible, nurturing, helpful,* and so on, should never be the sole basis upon which a person's performance is evaluated. Even though evaluating traits and dispositions is highly subjective, it can be useful in formative evaluation when multiple perspectives are included.

Performance criteria should include both inputs and outputs. While the terms *inputs* and *outputs* sound a bit like what you'd hear on the assembly line at a factory, they provide an easy way to differentiate between the things that teachers do—inputs—and the results or learning outcomes that children achieve—outputs. Traditionally, evaluation rating forms focused more on the tasks and activities of teachers rather than looking at evidence of what children have experienced or the developmental gains they have achieved.

This is starting to change as research confirms that certain instructional approaches have a more powerful impact on children's development. For example, teachers' use of effective question-asking strategies promotes growth in children's conceptual understanding. Likewise, teachers who use a rich and expansive vocabulary in their conversations with children can have a greater impact on their children's language development. Using criteria that focus on both inputs and outputs reinforces this important connection. The challenge, of course, is that children's learning is influenced by many other factors outside the teacher's control. Thus children's academic gains should never be used as the sole criteria upon which to evaluate performance.

The Value of Multiple Perspectives—A 360-Degree Approach

Multiple sources of evidence collected at multiple points during the year can improve the reliability of performance appraisal. In early childhood programs where directors often wear both hats—supervisor and evaluator—it is important to use multiple sources of evidence to assess teachers' performance. The kinds of evidence used in a comprehensive performance appraisal will be both formal and informal and include different stakeholders. The goal is to gather different types of evidence that provide a holistic view of a teacher's performance and professional growth during the year.

From a developmental perspective, how the components of a 360-degree approach are carried out will look quite different for new teachers just finishing their first year on the job than they do for veteran teachers who have been through the performance appraisal cycle multiple times. Seasoned teachers who are both competent and committed can take a self-directed approach in gathering data from multiple sources and preparing information for a performance appraisal meeting with you or their designated supervisor. In general, new teachers in your program, or teachers whose commitment to

Practice hands-off management as much as possible and hands-on management as much as necessary.

Ken Blanchard

their job is waning, will need a more directed approach by their supervisor in gathering relevant data and scheduling a meeting to go over the results.

Self-assessment. If you are serious about wanting to make the performance appraisal process meaningful, it is essential that you help teachers assess their own growth and performance. Perhaps the best way to accomplish this is with professional portfolios—a collection of reflections, artifacts, and relevant documents that capture a teacher's growth and professional achievements over time.

If your center doesn't have this practice in place already, don't be discouraged if 100% of your teachers don't enthusiastically jump on the bandwagon to get the process going. It can seem overwhelming at first. Begin with those who express interest, and provide them with the time needed to create and maintain their portfolio. As a starter, their portfolios can include a copy of their individual learning plans and evidence of the activities and outcomes described in their plans.

Help your teachers think of a professional portfolio as an organizer for learning. It can be as simple as an accordion file organizer in which they accumulate reflections, artifacts, and certificates, or as slick as a leather-bound binder with detailed inserts highlighting their professional journey and accomplishments. If they are whizzes at technology, they may prefer to use a digital format with selected items scanned and organized in an electronic template. Whatever the format, it should express each teacher's unique personality and sense of creativity.

The goal of using portfolios in the performance appraisal process is to help teachers think of their portfolio as a source of evidence of effective teaching and children's learning. Here are a few things they might include:

- Certificates of attendance from in-service workshops or professional conferences attended during the year

- Transcript of college courses completed

- Videotaped segments of classroom instruction

- Journal reflections of teachable moments they are most proud of

- Sample documentation of children's learning

- Photographs of the learning environment and daily activities that capture their core values

- Peer learning team reflections

- Examples of how children's assessment data is used to refine curriculum plans and scaffold children's learning

- A sample of their classroom newsletter

- Notes of appreciation from children, parents, and peers

- Summary reports of classroom observations conducted for QRIS

- An updated values and belief statement or educational philosophy

- Feedback from co-worker evaluations

The great thing about portfolios is that during your annual performance conversation with the teacher, the portfolio can serve as a springboard for discussion and help shift the control of the conversation from the supervisor to the teacher. Maintaining professional portfolios certainly takes time, but when done right, they serve as a dynamic, ever-changing reflection of a teacher's growth as an early childhood educator and a treasured memento as the teacher looks back on his or her teaching career.

Feedback from supervisor. As a supervisor, it's easy to come up with a litany of excuses to put off giving feedback to teachers: If we wait long enough the situation will resolve itself; we don't have time; we're not sure how the other person will react. Even sanitizing the diapering table seems more appealing than dealing with an uncomfortable confrontation with a low-performing teacher. As a result, we miss prime opportunities to exercise leadership and inspire peak performance. Providing meaningful feedback is integral to developing people.

Many directors argue that their seasoned teachers, their star performers, don't need feedback. After all, they're already performing at a high level. Research conducted by Finkelstein and Fishbach question the validity of this thinking. They underscore the importance of differentiating feedback for novice and seasoned employees. They found that positive feedback (*Here is what you did really well ...*) increases commitment by focusing on building experience and confidence. It is most effective for novice teachers. More detailed critical feedback (*Here's where things didn't go so well ...*) is informative and tells teachers where they need to expend more effort to improve. This kind of feedback is more effective with seasoned, high-performing teachers.

This makes sense. If you are a novice and you don't know what you are doing, positive feedback helps you stay optimistic and keep trying in the face of challenges. When you are an accomplished teacher and you already know what you are doing, it is critical feedback that can help you polish your craft.

If your center has implemented a developmental approach to supervision and teacher induction similar to what we describe in Chapters 3 and 4, your teachers are already receiving small but frequent doses of feedback from their supervisors. The most helpful feedback, as you have already learned, is tied to short, informal observations focusing on areas of classroom practice you and the teacher have targeted as important, along with your anecdotal notes about the teacher's instructional skills and level of attunement.

Data from periodic formal observations using assessments like the ECERS-R, CLASS, or ELLCO can also yield useful data, but we feel strongly that the data from these assessments should never be used as the single source of evidence in a high-stakes evaluation of a teacher's performance. They provide only a snapshot in time and may or may not be representative of the practices you have witnessed during the course of the year. These tools assess the classroom environment and teacher-child interactions of all members of the teaching team. They do not focus on a specific teacher. Likewise, the results of children's progress during the year, as measured by different assessments, can inform the discussion but should never be used as the sole criterion for evaluating performance.

Your goal in your summative annual performance evaluation is to assess the teacher's performance against the criteria that you and the teacher have agreed upon. Ideally these criteria should be tied to their job description or an established evaluation framework for teaching. If you need help getting started, the book *Blueprint for Action* provides an example of how a job description based on the CDA (Child Development Associate) competency standards can serve as a template for developing a performance appraisal form.

The Danielson Framework for Teaching is a popular evaluation template in elementary and secondary school settings. The criteria included in the framework relating to the components of professional practice—planning and preparation, the classroom environment, instruction, and professional responsibilities—can also serve as a source for developing your own performance appraisal form. Both the *Blueprint for Action* and Danielson examples include criteria that focus not just on how teachers perform in classroom, but also how they support the broader mission of the center and their demonstrated commitment to their own professional development.

Feedback from parents. Feedback from the parents or guardians of children provides another rich source of evidence of a teacher's performance. In addition to having teachers gather examples of parent notes and other correspondence that document their level of satisfaction and level of engagement in the life of the classroom, consider sending out a short questionnaire once a year to all the families enrolled in your center. The results can then be shared with each teacher. There are five areas of parent satisfaction you'll want to assess:

- Do parents feel they are regularly informed about their children's growth and development?

- Do teachers encourage families to be actively involved in their children's learning?

- Have parents had sufficient opportunity for informal conversations with teachers to gain insight into how their children are doing?

- How do parents feel their children have benefited from their experience in the classroom?

- Do parents and other family members feel they have had sufficient opportunity to be involved in classroom activities through volunteering, special projects, or sharing talents?

Don't be surprised if the feedback elicited from parents is quite diverse. This is to be expected, because different parents often have different expectations of what their children's educational experiences should be. You already know you will never be able to please all the families all the time, and you need to help teachers put the feedback from parents in perspective. Instead of perseverating on feedback from a single family, help teachers look for patterns in the responses to questions. These patterns can help identify areas of the teacher–family relationship that are strong and vibrant and areas that may need some extra attention.

Feedback from co-workers. Feedback from co-workers is another important source of data from which teachers can benefit. The two most frequent ways co-worker information is gathered is through peer observations conducted in the teacher's classroom and through a survey distributed to a sample of co-workers at the center. Because the broader goal of soliciting feedback from co-workers is to strengthen the collaborative culture of the center and reinforce norms of supporting each other's learning, the spirit in which co-worker data are gathered must always be cast as caring and helpful, never judging or critical. For that reason, it is important to use feedback from co-workers as a type of formative evaluation rather summative evaluation.

Peer observations can be informal or structured and as short as 10 minutes or as long as a few hours. They can be set up to focus on a narrow slice of the daily routine or be broad in scope, looking at different aspects of children's engagement in learning or the teacher's use of different instructional strategies. The following example of peer feedback illustrates how co-worker observations can serve to help a teacher validate what is going well and provide insight into an area of the children's learning experience that could be strengthened.

Peer Observation

Name of colleague observed: Barbara   **Date:** May 15

The focus of my observation today was on . . .
Children's use of different learning centers during morning free choice.

Aspects of this classroom I was impressed with include . . .

1. I loved the bookmaking materials that were available in your literacy area. The children really seemed to enjoy doing their story dictations with Samantha's grandmother. She is so patient with the children. What a gem!

2. The obstacle course was a real hit with the children in the gross motor area. I thought it might be too difficult for some of the younger children, but they seemed to like the challenge, particularly the limbo bar.

3. I like the fact that you don't overwhelm the children with too many things to investigate in your science center. The way the butterfly displays were organized helped focus the children's attention. It was great to see how you connected this science theme with your art project today.

Aspects of this classroom that might be strengthened include . . .

1. I noticed that when the children went back and forth from the butterfly art project to look at the butterfly pictures in the science area, they dripped paint along the way. Not sure how to solve this one, but perhaps you could laminate some of the butterfly pictures and bring them to the art area.

2. Both the obstacle course and the butterfly art project required a lot of adult supervision. It might be good in the future to schedule high-maintenance activities like this on different days.

3. Next time you do the obstacle course, let me know. I've got some great industrial cardboard tubes that might be fun to incorporate. I am happy to loan them to you.

Jesse

While only a few co-workers may have firsthand knowledge of a particular teacher's effectiveness in the classroom, most colleagues can readily offer feedback about how a teacher contributes to the collaborative culture of learning at the center. As with all feedback tools, involving staff in the development of the specific items will help ensure greater buy in. Appendix D, "Co-Worker Feedback Survey," is an example of a short questionnaire that can serve as an example in the design of your center's co-worker survey form.

After you've determined the items for your survey, you'll need to decide which staff should complete the survey for each teacher. Depending on the context of your setting, you may want to limit the feedback only to other teachers, or you may want to include feedback from administrative and support staff. Soliciting feedback from six to eight people is usually sufficient to give the teacher a sense of the multiple perspectives on the different behaviors and traits included.

Starting out, it is best to have staff complete your co-worker feedback survey anonymously. This means that you'll need to identify a neutral third party to summarize the data submitted for each teacher. At the end of the sample survey in Appendix D is a summary form. This can be used to determine the average rating for each item. The teacher can then be sent the average scores for each item along with the list of perceived strengths.

The best way to foster organizational norms that encourage staff to provide helpful feedback to one another is to model the approach yourself. Another book in the Director's Toolbox series, _Leadership in Action_, includes a multi-rater feedback survey that you can use to solicit feedback about your own performance. Not only will the results give you useful information about your strengths and areas to target for improvement, the process will reinforce the message that providing meaningful feedback is a leadership skill that can be practiced at every level of the organization. In doing so you'll be taking a bold step in creating your vision of a true professional learning community.

The Annual Performance Appraisal Conversation

Once a year you'll want to hold a summative performance appraisal conversation with each teacher. While most human resources guidebooks refer to this as a performance appraisal _conference,_ we prefer the term _conversation,_ keeping in line with the collaborative tone we've tried to communicate about the entire performance evaluation process.

This conversation should include a discussion about the outcomes of the teacher's individual learning plan and an appraisal of the teachers' overall performance during the year. Here are some questions you can ask your teachers to think about as they prepare for their performance conversation with you or their supervisor:

- What do you consider your most important accomplishments this past year?

- What did you learn this past year that you didn't know the previous year? How has this knowledge made you more effective in your work?

- Do you have the opportunity every day to do what you do best?

- If you could expand or enrich your job to more closely resemble your ideal, what resources or support would you need to make that happen?

- In what ways have you helped your colleagues become better at their jobs?

- In what ways have you added value to the center's reputation in the community?

This meeting provides an opportunity for teachers to go through the documentation they've assembled in their professional portfolio, share the insights they've gleaned from the parent and co-worker feedback they received, and review the ratings you've given them on their summative evaluation form.

"Just measuring your job performance."

There are two aspects of your role in this meeting that you'll want to keep in mind: the content or the information that you want to communicate and the tone or way you deliver the message. When the message may be perceived as negative or critical, think about the result you want from the exchange with the other person. This can help clarify in your mind how to frame both the content and the tone. It always helps to ask yourself first how you'd feel if someone gave you this feedback. If you would feel defensive or uncomfortable, you can probably assume the other person will too.

Performance appraisal will never be comfortable and routine for supervisors. There will always be challenging situations when your perceptions of teachers' performance differ from their perceptions. But remember, if your feedback is to be effective, it can't overwhelm. Think about the core message you want to communicate—the two or three things you want the teacher to remember months later. Try to present this information in a way that will be easy for the teacher to understand and translate into action.

Nurturing a Culture of Appreciation

While no one is thrilled to have their mistakes or shortcomings pointed out, it is also clear that constructive feedback is more readily received in organizations where employees feel they are respected and appreciated for their hard work. It's simple arithmetic. If the majority of messages people hear focus on their strengths and the value they add to the organization, then there is a greater likelihood they will exert more effort in their job. In research studies across occupations, workers indicate that feeling appreciated is as important in their overall job satisfaction as their paycheck. Your own experience probably bears this out.

Some social psychologists make the subtle distinction between *recognition*, which focuses primarily on performance or achievement of certain goals, and *appreciation*, which focuses on the value of the individual employee. Whichever lens you view it with, your employees need both. The Hawthorne effect is alive and well in our early childhood programs: recognizing people can boost their performance.

Whether recognition or appreciation, it needs to be genuine, delivered with a tone of sincerity. When possible, it should also be personalized. Some people love to be acknowledged in public for their accomplishments, while others prefer a handwritten note or small gift recognizing their efforts. The key is that the expression of appreciation must be viewed as valuable to the recipient in order to have an impact.

Extraordinary achievements never bloom in barren and unappreciative surroundings.

James Kouzes

One of the hallmarks of exemplary early childhood programs is that they nurture a culture of appreciation. In other words, they look for opportunities to regularly celebrate individual and group accomplishments. They recognize individual milestones, like employment anniversary dates or the certificates and degrees people achieve, and they celebrate centerwide accomplishments, like the attainment of accreditation or a QRIS rating.

Nurturing a culture of appreciation doesn't require a separate budget line item. It doesn't mean whisking your team away to a weekend spa retreat (although that would be nice). In fact it can be done without spending a penny. Saying the simple two-word expression, "Thank you," with genuine sincerity to recognize a job well done can communicate a lot. Equally powerful is the four-word question, "What do you think?," validating the importance of people's ideas.

Every person wants to feel significant; every person wants to know that they make a difference. Nurturing a culture of appreciation means that you have tapped into these two primal human needs. Isn't that worth pursuing? Seems like an important way to inspire peak performance.

A Final Word

We've had the good fortune to be able to visit hundreds of centers and meet with early childhood directors representing the amazing array of programs that make up our field—nonprofit and for-profit, part-day and full-day, Head Start, faith based, small mom-and-pop operations, and huge corporate-sponsored businesses. From our bird's eye view, it seems that directors can be divided into two camps—those who settle for "good enough," providing an acceptable level of education for children and decent working conditions for staff, and directors who "go for the gold," striving for excellence by inspiring peak performance.

What are the nuanced differences in leadership that distinguish good-enough programs from truly exemplary programs? What are the challenges that are bumps in the road for some directors but tire-popping potholes for others? There is no one-size-fits-all recipe for success, but one thing is certain—achieving an authentic professional learning community that inspires peak performance requires more than shouting your intentions from a mountaintop or hanging a motivational banner in your center's foyer.

We readily acknowledge that this type of comprehensive approach to professional development can feel overwhelming. That is why directors who are successful almost always have a strategic plan that maps out their intentions in small, actionable steps. This *kaizen* mindset is essential because approaching change in small, doable steps helps eliminate the fear and resistance that are byproducts of the change process.

So stepping back and looking at the big picture of how your program is currently functioning, what one or two strategies in this book might you consider introducing in your program first? What small steps can you take today that will help strengthen competence, commitment, and collaboration?

As you move forward, think of the organizational systems you need to put in place to create and sustain your vision. Good systems are essential for gathering data about performance and ensuring there is a systematic cycle of reflection and feedback that supports continuous quality improvement. A good resource for helping you think about the essential systems you need is the *Program Administration Scale*, more commonly referred to as the PAS. The human resources development subscale in the PAS includes items relating to staff orientation, supervision, performance appraisal, and staff development—all essential components of a professional learning community.

Is achieving a professional learning community at your center realistic in the real world of early care and education—a world where low standards, low wages, and tight resources fuel high turnover? The answer, as you'd probably expect us to say, is, "Absolutely! Yes!" Even in a work context where it seems like the human resource cards are stacked against you, it is possible to strengthen competence, commitment, and collaboration if you match high expectations with high levels of support. You set the tone; your words and your actions encourage or stifle experimentation and your teachers' willingness to look at their classroom practices and their own learning in new and innovative ways.

Imagine going for the gold because the children, families, and teachers in your center deserve it, and you have the leadership capacity and vision to make it happen. We wish you much success inspiring peak performance.

One of the great things an organization can do is to help people give voice to their dreams, and provide the means by which people can come together to create something greater than themselves. It is the gift of leaders to release the aspirations of others.

James Champy

For Further Reading

Albrecht, K. (2002). *The right fit: Recruiting, selecting, and orienting staff*. Lake Forest, IL: New Horizons.

Albrecht, K., & Engel, B. (2007). Moving away from a quick-fix mentality to systematic professional development. *Young Children, 62*(4), 18–25.

Allensworth, E. M., Ponisciak, S., & Mazzeo, C. (2009). *The schools teachers leave: Teacher mobility in Chicago public schools*. Chicago: Consortium on Chicago School Research.

Bearwald, R. (2011, October). It's about the questions. *Educational Leadership, 69*(2), 74–77.

Bella, J. (2008, July/Aug). Improving leadership and management practices: One step at a time. *Exchange*, 6–9.

Biddle, J. K. (2012). *The three Rs of leadership: Building effective early childhood programs through relationships, reciprocal learning, and reflection*. Ypsilanti, MI: HighScope.

Bloom, P. J. (2013). *Leadership in action: How effective directors get things done* (2nd ed.). Lake Forest, IL: New Horizons.

Bloom, P. J. (2007). *From the inside out: The power of reflection and self-awareness*. Lake Forest, IL: New Horizons.

Bloom, P. J. (2005). *Blueprint for action: Achieving center-based change through staff development* (2nd ed.). Lake Forest, IL: New Horizons.

Bowman, B. (2006, September). Standards at the heart of educational equity. *Young Children, 61*(5), 42–48.

Buckingham, M. (2007). *Go put your strengths to work*. New York: Free Press.

Carter, M. (2010, July/August). Drive-through training. *Exchange*, 61–63.

Carter, M., & Curtis, D. (2010). *The visionary director: A handbook for dreaming, organizing, and improvising in your center* (2nd ed.). St. Paul, MN: Redleaf.

Caruso, J. J., & Fawcett, M. T. (2007). *Supervision in early childhood: A developmental perspective* (3rd ed.). New York: Teachers College Press.

Cheliotes, L. G., & Reilly, M. F. (2012). *Opening the door to coaching conversations*. Thousand Oaks, CA: Corwin.

Cook, M. J. (2011). *Effective coaching* (2nd ed.). New York: McGraw Hill.

Curtis, D., Lebo, D., Cividanes, W., & Carter, M. (2013). *Reflecting in communities of practice: A workbook for early childhood educators*. St. Paul, MN: Redleaf.

Danielson, C. (2007). *Enhancing professional practice: A framework for teaching*. Alexandria, VA: Association for the Supervision and Curriculum Development.

Danielson, C., & McGreal, T. (2000). *Teacher evaluation to enhance professional practice*. Alexandria, VA: Association for Supervision and Curriculum Development.

Deviney, J., Duncan, S., Harris, S., Rody, M., & Rosenberry, L. (2010). *Inspiring spaces for young children*. Silver Spring, MD: Gryphon House.

Deviney, J., Duncan, S., Harris, S., Rody, M., & Rosenberry, L. (2010). *Rating Observation Scale for Inspiring Environments*. Silver Spring, MD: Gryphon House.

Dombro, A., Jablon, J., & Stetson, C. (2013, March/April). Using powerful interactions with colleagues to promote powerful interactions with children. *Exchange*, 75–77.

DuFour, R., & Fullan, M. (2013). *Cultures built to last: Systemic PLCs at work*. Bloomington, IN: Solution Tree.

DuFour, R., DuFour R., Eaker, R., & Many, T. (2010). *Learning by doing: A handbook for professional learning communities at work*. Bloomington, IN: Solution Tree.

Eaker, R., & Keating, J. (2008, Summer). A shift in school culture. *Journal of Staff Development, 29*(3), 14–17.

Epstein, A. (2007). *The intentional teacher: Choosing the best strategies for young children's learning*. Washington, DC: NAEYC.

Feiman-Nemser, S. (2003, May). What new teachers need to learn. *Educational Leadership. 60*(8), 25–29.

Finkelstein, S. R., & Fishbach, A. (2012, June). Tell me what I did wrong. Experts respond to negative feedback. *Journal of Consumer Research, 39*, 22–38.

Glickman, C. D., Gordon, S., & Ross-Gordon, J. (2013). *Supervision and instructional leadership: A developmental approach* (9th ed.). Boston: Pearson.

Guernsey, L., & Ochshorn, S. (2011, November). *Watching teachers work: Using observation tools to promote effective teaching in the early years and early grades.* Washington, DC: The New America Foundation, Early Education Initiative.

Guss, S., Horm, D., & Lang, E. (2013, July). Using classroom quality assessments to inform teacher decisions. *Young Children, 68*(3), 16–20.

Hallowell, E. (2011). *Shine: Using brain science to get the best from your people.* Boston, MA: Harvard Business Review Press.

Hargreaves, A. (1994). *Changing teachers; changing times.* New York: Teachers College Press.

Harms, T., Clifford, R., & Cryer, D. (2005). *Early Childhood Environment Rating Scale–Revised.* New York: Teachers College Press.

Heller, S. S., & Gilkerson, L. (Eds.). (2011). *A practical guide to reflective supervision.* Washington, DC: Zero to Three.

Intrator, S. M., & Kunzman, R. (2006, March). Starting with the soul. *Educational Leadership, 63*(6), 38–42.

Jones, E. (1993). *Growing teachers: Partnerships in staff development.* Washington, DC: NAEYC.

Joseph, G. E., Sandall, S. R., Porter, A., Lane, V., Shapiro, R., & Nolen, E. (2011, October). *School readiness for all children: Using data to support child outcomes.* Seattle, WA: National Center on Quality Teaching & Learning in Head Start, University of Washington. Retrieved from www. hitinc.org/uploads%5Cresources%5C1308%5Cncqtl_data_handbook_version_ 11_1_11.pdf

Katz, L. (1972). Developmental stages of preschool teachers. *Elementary School Journal, 73*, 50–55.

Katz, L. (1993). *Dispositions: Definitions and implications for early childhood practices.* Urbana, IL: ERIC Clearinghouse on Elementary and Early Childhood Education.

Katz, L. (1993). *Helping others with their teaching*. Urbana, IL: ERIC Clearinghouse on Elementary and Early Childhood Education.

Kegan, R. (2000). What "form" transforms? A constructive-developmental approach to transformative learning. In J. Mezirow (Ed.), *Learning as transformation* (pp. 35–69). San Francisco: Jossey-Bass.

Killion, J. (2013). *Meet the promise of content standards: Taping technology to enhance professional learning*. Oxford, OH: Learning Forward.

Kise, J. (June, 2012). Giving teams a running start: Take steps to build shared vision, trust, and collaboration skills, *Journal of Staff Development, 33*(3), 38–42.

Kohn, A. (2001, September). Five reasons to stop saying "Good Job!" *Young Children, 56*(5), 24–28.

Kruger, J., & Dunning, D. (1999). Unskilled and unaware of it: How difficulties in recognizing one's own incompetence lead to inflated self-assessments. *Journal of Personality and Social Psychology, 77*(6), 1121–33.

Lawrence-Lightfoot, S. (1983). *The good high school: Portraits of character and culture*. New York: Basic Books.

Leana, C., Appelbaum, E., & Shevchuk, I. (2009). Work process and quality of care in early childhood education: The role of job crafting. *Academy of Management Journal, 52*(6), 1169–92.

Lipton, L., & Wellman, B. (2012). *Got data? Now what? Creating and leading cultures of inquiry*. Bloomington, IN: Solution Tree Press.

Little, J. W. (1982). Norms of collegiality and experimentation: Workplace conditions of school success. *American Educational Research Journal, 19*, 325–40.

McDonald, J., Mohr, N., Dichter, A., & McDonald, E. (2007). *The power of protocols* (2nd ed.). New York: Teachers College Press.

Maurer, R. (2004). *One small step can change your life: The Kaizen way*. New York: Workman.

National Association for the Education of Young Children and National Association of Early Childhood Specialists in State Departments of Education. (2002). *Early learning standards: Creating the conditions for success. Joint position statement*. www.naeyc.org/positionstatements/learning-standards.

Palmer, P. (2003, Summer). Honor the human heart. *Journal of Staff Development, 24*(3), 49–54.

Pelo, A. (2006, November/December). Growing a culture of inquiry: Observation as professional development. *Exchange*, 50–53.

Pianta, R., LaParo, K., & Hamre, B. (2007). *Classroom Assessment Scoring System.* Baltimore, MD: Brookes.

Pink, D. (2009). *Drive: The surprising truth about what motivates us.* New York: Riverhead Books.

Smith, M., & Brady, J. (2008). *Early Language and Literacy Classroom Observation Pre-K Tool.* Baltimore, MD: Brookes.

Sugarman, N. A. (2011). Putting yourself in action: Individual professional development plans. *Young Children, 66*(3), 27–33.

Talan, T. N. (2010, May/June). Distributed leadership: Something new or something borrowed? *Exchange*, 8–12.

Talan, T. N., & Bloom, P. J. (2011). *Program Administration Scale: Measuring leadership and management in early childhood* (2nd ed.). New York: Teachers College Press.

Vygotsky, L. S. (1978). *Mind and society: The development of higher psychological processes.* Cambridge, MA: Harvard University Press.

Wiggins, G. (2012, September). 7 keys to effective feedback. *Educational Leadership, 70*(1), 11–16.

Winton, P., McCollum, J., & Catlett, C. (2008). *Practical approaches to early childhood professional development.* Washington, DC: Zero to Three.

Wood, F. H., & McQuarrie, F. (1999, Summer). On-the-job learning. *Journal of Staff Development*, 10–13.

Video Clips

www.highscope.org/Content.asp?ContentId=381
HighScope offers a limited number of video clips that are available to anyone, but the full library of web clips is available to members only. Membership is free.

www.illinoisearlylearning.org/videos/
The Illinois Early Learning Project provides video clips with background information, a transcript, and a description of how various benchmarks are met.

videatives.com/blog/archives/
Videatives offers over 300 video clips about early education to increase understanding of children's thinking and learning.

www.cde.state.co.us/resultsmatter/RMVideoSeries_ PracticingObservation.htm#top
The Colorado Department of Education provides a Results Matter video library for early childhood professional development activities.

www.teachstone.org/professional-development/
For a subscription fee, you have access to hundreds of classroom videos focused on teacher–child interactions that support learning.

Focused Observations
This publication by G. Gronlund and M. James includes an interactive CD-ROM with 19 vignettes of children in action. It is published by Redleaf Press.

Appendices

Leadership as an Organizational Asset

In high-performing organizations, leadership skills and competencies are widely held by staff regardless of role or title. This inventory will help you assess whether specific skills or competencies are displayed by a few or by many in the center.

Leadership skill or competency	Exhibited by...	
The ability to...	*a few*	*many*
• listen attentively and respectfully		
• ask thoughtful questions that expand other people's understanding of an issue		
• understand another person's point of view and unique perspective		
• facilitate a meeting, providing a balance between getting business done and encouraging full participation		
• write a concise, persuasive document that clearly communicates information to the intended audience		
• make a presentation that clearly communicates necessary information on an issue or topic		
• keep informed about new trends in the field		
• synthesize important information from documents and reports		
• make decisions based on relevant data and consider the consequences of those decisions for different stakeholders		
• stay on task with a project, from initial conceptualization of the idea through implementation and evaluation of the outcomes		
• provide feedback to others in a direct, respectful, and supportive manner		
• complete high-priority tasks with the effective use of time		
• organize space and materials to facilitate the efficient use of time		
• show concern and empathy for others, with an appropriate level of emotion		
• defuse conflict by resolving complaints and grievances in a professional manner		
• intervene to stop gossip		
• collect and analyze data to benchmark program improvement efforts		
• ask challenging questions without putting the person on the defensive		

Bloom, P. J., Hentschel, A., Bella, J. (2013). *Inspiring Peak Performance*. Lake Forest, IL: New Horizons. (www.newhorizonsbooks.net)

Individual Learning Plan

Teacher's name _____   Date _____

Self-Reflection

What aspect of your job gives you the greatest personal satisfaction?

What aspect of your job is most frustrating?

What keeps you from being as effective as you would like to be in your position?

If you had the power to change anything about your job, what would you change?

What do you see yourself doing five years from now?

What new skills or knowledge would you like to learn this year?

How can I or other staff help you achieve your personal and professional goals?

Goal Setting

Strengths as a teacher

1. _____

2. _____

3. _____

Identified growth areas

1. _____

2. _____

3. _____

Goal _____

_____

Related standards _____

_____

Objectives

1. _____

2. _____

3. _____

Action Steps

Objective #1: _____

Activities	Time needed	Resources needed

Evaluation: _____

Objective #2: _____

Activities	Time needed	Resources needed

Evaluation: _____

Objective #3: _____

Activities	Time needed	Resources needed

Evaluation: _____

Bloom, P. J., Hentschel, A., Bella, J. (2013). *Inspiring Peak Performance.* Lake Forest, IL: New Horizons. (www.newhorizonsbooks.net)

Getting to Know the Assessment Tool

Teacher: Date:

Assessment tool:

Item or dimension:

_____

Why does this item matter for positive child outcomes?

Key questions prompted by the item	The environment includes	A child will experience
•	•	•
•	•	•
•	•	•

When you think about this item in your own environment, what questions come up?

What steps are necessary to implement or improve this item in your environment?

Bloom, P. J., Hentschel, A., Bella, J. (2013). _Inspiring Peak Performance._ Lake Forest, IL: New Horizons. (www.newhorizonsbooks.net)